A Toolkit for Provosts

A Toolkit for Provosts

A Series of Real Stories and Case Studies

Patricia Mosto, Gail Simmons, Brian McGee, and Dianne Dorland

ROWMAN & LITTLEFIELD
Lanham • Boulder • New York • London

Published by Rowman & Littlefield
An imprint of The Rowman & Littlefield Publishing Group, Inc.
4501 Forbes Boulevard, Suite 200, Lanham, Maryland 20706
www.rowman.com

6 Tinworth Street, London SE11 5AL, United Kingdom

British Library Cataloguing in Publication Information Available

Library of Congress Cataloging-in-Publication Data

Library of Congress Control Number: 2020938706

ISBN 978-1-4758-4807-6 (cloth)
ISBN 978-1-4758-4808-3 (paperback)
ISBN 978-1-4758-4809-0 (electronic)

♾™ The paper used in this publication meets the minimum requirements of American National Standard for Information Sciences—Permanence of Paper for Printed Library Materials, ANSI/NISO Z39.48-1992.

Contents

Acknowledgments

We are grateful to the many colleagues who provided ideas and recommended content areas for this book. We have chosen not to name them to protect their anonymity, but they know who they are. Many of those colleagues, mostly current or past provosts, have provided useful feedback on earlier drafts of this book.

Also, thanks to Rowman and Littlefield, especially Tom Koerner under whom this project began, and Carlie Wall for editing assistance.

When this book project was initiated, two of the four coauthors were sitting provosts. By the time the manuscript was in final revisions, both sitting provosts had made career changes. One had returned to faculty life after a long and rewarding administrative career, while the other had moved to a presidency. These personal transitions are reminders of the many options available to provosts, and we believe the current book provides multiple and useful perspectives on those options.

Finally, we are deeply indebted to our friends and families for their patience and support during the many hours we spent on this book.

Preface

What inspired us to write this book? All of us, current or past provost or associate provost, have been interested in learning about higher administration. Our life paths have echoed with many provosts across the country. As there are very few books for provosts, we wanted to share ours and others' provost stories that we think will help to shape your path to a provostship.

Provosts are both the managers and the leaders of Academic Affairs units, and most times the second-in-command at their universities. Leading is providing direction, implementing plans, and motivating people. Managing is implementing policies, administering budgets, and addressing requests from the president and other administrators.

As a way to address the myriad range of challenges a provost faces, and the variations at different institutions, we wrote personal stories and case studies. They serve as learning tools for seeing how others have solved problems and dealt with situations. We found it useful to think about problems or situations beforehand and hear how others have handled them, even if our eventual choices were different.

When analyzing the personal stories and case studies, the reader should identify those aspects of the settings that apply to their own institutions. While there will be differences in the determination of who was involved, what actions they take, the cost of those actions, the outcomes achieved, and what information was available, the readers will find multiple connectors to provide insights to their own situations.

The personal stories and case studies highlight particular issues related to the chapter content. These personal stories and case studies are intended to connect theory to concrete issues, to encourage further thinking, and to facilitate discussion.

The personal stories and case studies in this book are based on a range of experiences, ours as well as other provosts and associate provosts, from a variety of institutional sizes and locations, including both privates and public universities. We have changed names and details, and used gender pronouns alternately to avoid identification of any real situation.

We hope that this book will be useful, especially if you are a new provost, although every provost may find new insight with these personal stories and case studies.

Introduction

The leader is one who, out of the clutter, brings simplicity . . . out of discord, harmony . . . and out of difficulty, opportunity.

—Albert Einstein

A question that always arises in conversation among academicians is who wants to be a provost and why? And what does a provost do anyway? The position of a provost varies at different universities. In some, the provost will lead all of those areas that directly touch the delivery of instruction—she will be the "Dean of Deans" and also oversee academic advising, the libraries, and the academic records unit. Some will have duties that encompass continuing education and career services, or even information technology (IT).

In other cases the role will be more narrowly focused, and in some smaller institutions the provost role will include being "Dean of the Faculty" in the absence of deans. In the end, provosts need to deal with institutional challenges, critical issues, a never-ending shortfall of resources, conflicts, and most draining, difficult personnel issues. In most institutions, the provost is considered "first among equals" among his/her vice presidential colleagues.

In an era when the nature of pedagogy is being challenged, rethought, expanded, digitized, and personalized, provosts may also find themselves in the position of "Chief Learning Officer," advocating for the use of new tools, new strategies, and new viewpoints on teaching and learning to faculty, deans, presidents, information technologists, librarians, and students.

The first use of the title provost in American higher education is unclear. At the University of Pennsylvania, the title provost dates to the late eighteenth century. Before the 1930s, the administrative head of the university was titled provost. In the 1930s, the board of trustees (BoT) created a separate office of the president and redesignated the provost as the chief academic officer, subordinate to the presidency.

In other American universities and colleges, the provost position was created during and after World War II when dramatic increases in undergraduate enrollments were seen. With growing enrollments and the increased complexity of higher education administration, many chief executive officers were led to adopt a more corporate governing structure. By the 1960s, most of the Ivy League institutions had provosts (or equivalents), as did other private research universities.

A provost's life is always a learning opportunity. This learning comes from the different disciplines a provost leads (outside her/his own), the different business functions a provost executes, the challenges and opportunities a provost encounters, the people and personalities a provost manages, and the political machinations a provost impacts. The longevity of a provost job is estimated at 4.7 years.

As the chief academic officer, the provost is embedded in the complex and layered texture of the university, sees from afar the work of the faculty, and is a key player in the shared governance process and academic planning.

Although presidents set the broad institutional agenda, provosts, in general, identify and manage the agenda pieces that merge with the institutional mission and the time frames for change. Provosts are key in making their universities dynamic places that generate and respond to new ideas, directions, and possibilities. The provost, along with the deans and the faculty leadership, must continually encourage and support the units under her/his responsibility to move the university forward in a viable and effective manner.

This viable and effective manner needs to take into consideration the unintended consequences of new policies, people's reactions to change, and the economic implications of new policy applications. Furthermore, the leadership of an academic institution needs to put the university in a national and global context. As such, provosts need to place the institutional challenges and opportunities on the overall economic and political landscape.

In twenty-first-century America, a provost is often hired to be a change agent. In the face of a rapidly changing landscape for higher education, with multiple institutional threats arising from federal and state governments, economic pressures, public skepticism about the role of higher education and society, provosts are often seen as those who can help a college or university respond to these pressures.

Yet most provosts would agree that the academy is a highly conservative institution and that making change at a college or university is more like changing the course of an aircraft carrier than sailing a yacht. Change agency and change management are among the trickiest and most vitally important parts of the job of a provost.

There is no "school for provosts,"[1] so most learn "on the job." With very few guides for provosts, we wanted to share our thoughts and other provosts' stories as we think it may help to shape your path to a "provostship." That is what inspired us to write this book. Dr. McGee and Dr. Simmons are both former provosts. Dr. Mosto, as a dean and prior associate provost, has always been interested in higher administration issues, as it is the case with Dr. Dorland, a former dean. Our life paths have aligned with provosts across the country.

Provosts are both the managers and the leaders of academic affairs units and frequently the second-in-command at their universities. Leaders provide direction, implement plans, and motivate people. Managers implement policies, administer budgets, and address requests from the president and other administrators.

The personal stories and case studies in this book attempt to address the myriad range of challenges a provost faces, as well as any variations in these challenges that may occur at different institutions. The case studies and stories in this book come from individuals who are serving or who have served in the role of provost across institutional type and offer solutions on dealing with specific situations as well as provide advice on leadership approaches. We found it useful to structure the content around problems or situations others and we have encountered and hear how these issues were handled, even if the eventual choices were different.

When analyzing the personal stories and case studies, the reader should identify those aspects of the settings that apply to their own institutions. While there will be differences in the determination of who was involved, what information was available, what actions they took, the cost of those actions, and the outcomes achieved, the readers will find multiple connections to provide insights into their own situations.

During the so-called honeymoon period, provosts may have almost-perfect days, filled with interesting new people, challenging and yet exciting ideas, and a myriad of amazing opportunities. Those "perfect" days don't come too often, and they seem to fade too quickly, as provosts get to know their colleagues; challenging ideas do not materialize and opportunities are not fulfilled. What a provost can accomplish in the "honeymoon period" could be how s/he sets the agenda for their term as provost. Some of the personal stories and case studies in chapter 3 will give you insight into those "perfect" days.

---

[1] However, some higher education groups offer workshops and institutes to help new provosts learn their jobs. These include the American Council on Education's (ACE) Advancing to the Chief Academic Office Workshop and Institute for New Chief Academic Officers, and the Council of Independent Colleges' (CIC) Institute for Chief Academic Officers. The Association of Chief Academic Officers (ACAO) offers programming in conjunction with the annual meeting of the ACE.

Provosts are placed in a dual advocacy role; they take faculty and deans' issues up to their president and fellow vice presidents (VPs), and bring larger institutional concerns and realities down to the academic division. Negotiating with other higher administrators may require some astute psychology and understanding of human motivation, emotions, and responses to ideas and issues. Provosts are the face of academic affairs; they need to be prepared to be visible at events and represent the president.

Besides the president, probably the provost's most important ally is the chief financial officer (CFO), and when provosts and CFOs are on the same page, the possibilities of actions on part of the provost are enhanced. The chapter on how to negotiate with your president and other VPs is full of stories and case studies from many fellow provosts on this subject.

Most successful provosts are those who have a strong and reliable team, composed primarily of the associate provosts and deans. Universities are about people, their morale, and their pride. A successful provost is one who understands people and creates a strong team. Provosts have little time to do their work, so surrounding oneself with great staff that you trust in the delegation of responsibilities as well as trust the recommendations they provide creates a strong academic affairs division for the institution. In the chapter on the "provost's team," the personal stories and cases speak to the self-knowledge to trust one's own judgment and have the confidence to delegate and share the responsibilities of the job.

Most provosts establish their early careers in specific disciplines within a professional field. The transition to chief academic officer with oversight for all disciplines represents a challenge in both understanding and giving credibility to others in different disciplines. Provosts need to have the interest and capacity to learn, appreciate, and communicate in a full array of disciplines, and to accord those disciplines great respect.

The chapters in the book related to the academic division and faculty provide personal stories and cases on how provosts have dealt with many different disciplines and how to inspire the faculty they lead. Good provosts are curious, imaginative, and comfortable in the world outside their own area of expertise.

Before you delve into the book, we want to provide you with some thoughts about being a provost:

- *Respect your institution's processes*

  Each institution has its own processes; be respectful and knowledgeable of them. In university settings, hardly anything gets done on schedule. Be wary of process, and foster positive change without shortcutting. Understand your institution's appetite for risk: some presidents and boards have a great appetite for change, and for taking risks to make change, while others will be wary of new directions. In general, the faculty as a whole tends to push back against change, although individual faculty may present exciting ideas. Managing change processes both up to the president and down to the faculty is a large proportion of the creative work of a provost.

- *Understand the provost's responsibilities*

    Remember that you are now the person who takes care of business. Your job is to stay at the campus and run it. You must reorient your interests away from your discipline and toward the university as a whole. Political decisions can get you in trouble, so be careful.

- *Act transparently*

    Promote a climate of dialogue and be clear about why you do what you do. Answer questions honestly and completely. Speak from your heart and your mind, not from remarks someone else made. Be clear, honest, and complete.

- *Don't take it personally*

    The provost is the number two at any university, so the job is to never upstage the president and always speak for her/him. Remember that negative responses and disappointments following your actions are not about you as a person, but you in the role of a provost.

- *Time is your friend, so review and reflect before responding*

    Don't act upon the first compelling story you hear, as there are always competing stories. Never act rashly on a reported "crisis." Wait and gather all the pertinent information, consult colleagues who have had experience in similar situations, and then take a reasonable time before making a decision. Accurate notes will provide you with a clear picture after you gather data from different sources over a period of time.

- *People matter most*

    Each person at the university is part of its mission; respect everyone for their contributions. Give people your time and attention without interruption. They will love you!

- *Faculty are the capital of the university*

    The provost is the negotiator between the faculty's personal interest and the academic interests. Love your faculty; they do the real work of the university. Praise your faculty; they like to hear that you value their teaching, service, and scholarship. Build trust with your faculty, but don't expect them to know what goes on with the rest of the university or the academy as a whole. It's not their job; it's the way it is.

- *Pay attention to students*

    Whenever you are asked, show up. Students will love you for it. Be wary of only paying attention to the smart, talented, and assertive students. Most students are average, and they also look at you as their provost.

- *Space is the university's biggest problem*

  Universities may manage money well, but not space. Remember that space is distributed, occupied, and used, which leads to a feeling of ownership. "Do faculty own their offices?" They think so, but they don't. The university owns all spaces, and you are part of a team responsible for making the best use of space for the good of all. If your faculty believe their offices are part of their academic freedom, bring them to reality, but do it gently. Expect territoriality from everyone. On the topic of space, there are no friends.

- *Money is the winner*

  Unfortunately, money trumps over academics, curricular matters, or research. Your best strategy is to use money to modify behavior and get things done. Generally, the CFO is your best friend, and it's your job to keep it that way, so "take your CFO to lunch." Strategic allocation of funds seems to be the best indication that a strategy will get implemented. Nonstrategic allocation of resources (be it money, time, or space), or allocations that appear to be the result of "back room deals" can tie up resources in ways that can paralyze your institution.

Your ethical boundaries are bound to be challenged. It is impossible to serve as provost without eventually being confronted with a situation in which ethics and expediency collide. Much creative but unsung work of provosts involves finding a "third path" that preserves both the ethical core of the institution (and the provost's personal ethics) and still allows forward movement or a positive outcome. Yet provosts (for that matter, most anyone in a leadership role) must always be prepared for a day when they may need to consider resignation as an alternative to unethical behavior.

It is worth spending time, as you read these cases or current news stories about challenges in higher education to decide where your own "uncrossable lines" may lie. Doing so as you begin may save you from a great deal of soul-searching later. Finally, although job-related experience is of great importance, the mindset that provosts bring to the table, especially respect for the position, the academy, and a deep understanding and appreciation of the work of the faculty, is sometimes most important.

At the end of each chapter we have incorporated "food for thought," either leadership quotes we find appropriate and inspiring or our own thoughts in the matter on the chapter. We hope you enjoy reading this book and get some good ideas to help you in your job as provost.

Chapter 1

Preparing for the Provost Position

This chapter is a collection of personal stories about how we prepare ourselves to land a provost position. It discusses issues around the search process, the interview process, assessing the "right fit," and preparing for the campus interviews. In addition, we will consider the pros and cons of accepting a provost position from a personal and family perspective, such as relocation, salary, and career trajectory.

CASE 1: HOW I WEIGHED THE DECISION TO BECOME A PROVOST

Dr. Abba, a faculty member at a community college, was contemplating a move to a provost position after he was offered the post. Some people were telling him that it's a shame that the best and brightest have to abandon the classroom in order to be adequately compensated. Others were telling him that administrators are rarely the best and brightest.

But to Dr. Abba no one can dispute the obvious—administrators, as a rule, make a lot more money than faculty. Was money the best reason to go into an upper administration position? The answer was easy—of course, it's not. The best reason for Dr. Abba was that he was an obsessive-compulsive Type A personality, but earning more money was not a bad runner-up.

Considering a move to a provost's position, Dr. Abba weighed a number of factors besides salary. The first thing was that he knew that being a provost is hard work. He thought it might be accurate to say that being a provost (or any upper administrator for that matter) was more stressful and carried greater responsibility than being a faculty member.

There wasn't necessarily more to do, in fact, at times Dr. Abba thought administrators have less to do than faculty, but what they do is ultimately of greater consequence. By thinking that, Dr. Abba didn't disparage the work of the faculty. He was simply acknowledging that while faculty may be responsible for 100 or 200 students, provosts control the fate of thousands.

On top of that, Dr. Abba considered all the personnel matters—hiring, firing, evaluation, promotion, and tenure—for which, as a provost, along with department heads and deans, he was going to be largely responsible on his campus. He knew that if he failed in some of those decisions, he would come to know the true meaning of misery.

And then he also knew about the often false sense of urgency that attends everything a provost does. As a professor, Dr. Abba could pace himself throughout the week, perhaps grading twenty papers a day, for instance. As a provost, he wouldn't have that luxury. If the president or the chancellor needs something from the provost, they need it right now.

So Dr. Abba thought a lot before taking the position. He knew that being a provost, if not more labor intensive than teaching, was certainly more stressful. Many of his capable colleagues never bothered making the move into upper administration for precisely that reason; they didn't want the hassle. Others, after a short attempt, simply decided that the extra stress was not worth the additional cash. That was something he needed to think about before he accepted the position.

Another thing Dr. Abba knew is that a provost's job can be extremely tedious: interminable meetings, multiple and duplicative forms, mind-numbing reports, stacks of documents, and redundant evaluations. Even worse, perhaps, was what he knew about the not-so-busy times. Dr. Abba had many colleagues in provost positions. In fact, one of the worst things about being a provost was that one of his friends shared that she needed to be in her office from 8 a.m. to 5 p.m. every day, whether she had anything administrative to do or not.

Dr. Abba was very efficient when it came to paperwork, so he figured that if he took the position, once in a while, there would be days with no meetings where he could finish everything before noon. But he also knew that as a professor he could simply leave at that point. As a provost he couldn't. He knew that for a provost, simply being there is a large part of the job.

Dr. Abba also needed to weigh the pros in taking the position. Many of the positives were obvious, like money, prestige, and a degree of control. But some weren't. A great source of satisfaction, he knew, lies in knowing that he would have played a role in making the college a better place for everyone.

Believe it or not, among the long list of committees on which he had served over the years are some that actually performed good and useful work, such as the calendar committee that revamped the summer schedule to create longer breaks or the committee that helped design classrooms for a new building.

Dr. Abba had served as a faculty member on such committees, but he knew that as a provost he would get to do it more often. With so many committee assignments, some of them were bound to be worthwhile.

Keeping these pros and cons in mind, Dr. Abba accepted the provost position on his campus. Two-year colleges need good provosts as much as they need good teachers, and the former, in his experience, was much harder to find.

Questions

1. What do you think of Dr. Abba's decision?
2. Would you have taken the job? If so, why?
3. Was Dr. Abba right on his assessment of the position he was going to take?
4. Do you think money is a valid motivator for someone taking an upper administration position?

The Interview Process

The interview is perhaps the most influential factor in the academic employment process. Although curriculum vitae, cover letters, nominations, and recommendations are essential aspects that typically determine whether you will be invited for an interview, the on-site interview is generally the final determining factor in the selection process. Hence, during the interview process, you should convey not only academic and professional strengths but also collegiality in an appropriate manner.

Asking appropriate questions during interviews is essential in that it allows you to detect what is expected and also provides you with valuable information to determine if this position is a best fit for you.

Here we provide some framework for those of you seeking a provost position for asking questions during the interview process. We hope that these questions will help you with the interview as a two-way process in which both parties assume the joint role of interviewer and interviewee.

Questions posed by you play a crucial role in the interview process. First and foremost, good questions enable you to obtain information that you could not obtain directly from the institution's website. Second, good questions give a clear message to interviewers that you have prepared extremely well for the interview by meticulously reading all available information, which demonstrates your interest in and enthusiasm for the position. Third, good questions allow you to probe more deeply into certain issues pertaining to the unit, thereby enabling them to determine whether your leadership meets their needs.

You should use both closed-ended and open-ended questions. Closed-ended questions typically are asked for the purpose of obtaining specific information from faculty and administrators. In contrast, open-ended questions are asked for the purpose of obtaining broader information, as well as for obtaining information about perceptions, beliefs, and experiences. Basically there are three types of questions: main questions, probing questions, and follow-up questions.

Follow-up questions are specific to the previous comments made by the interviewers. These questions are essential for obtaining depth and detail, as well as for obtaining more nuanced answers. Follow-up questions can take various forms, including comparison questions, specific questions, general questions, and challenge questions.

Probing questions are questions asked to keep a discussion going while providing clarification. These questions help interviewers to continue talking on the topic at hand, expand on an idea, complete a missing piece of information, or to request clarification of what was stated. Moreover, by asking probing questions you can prevent the interviewer(s) from not providing sufficient detail. Some types of probing questions are explanatory probing, clarification probing, elaboration probing, continuation probing, steering probing, and in-depth, iterative probing.

You should refrain from asking leading questions, multiple questions, long-winded or complex questions, and questions that generate yes or no responses. Also, you should avoid using the word "Why" in your questions because it might unnecessarily put the interviewer(s) on the defensive. Further, you should avoid critiquing any responses or completing the interviewer's response.

Below we provide a list of possible questions you can ask:

1. What are the teaching expectations for a provost?
2. What are the expectations of the campus with respect to research?
3. What scope is there for me to write grants? And what support is available to assist me in writing grants?
4. Would I be able to attend the most relevant annual professional meetings in my field? Are there other professional meetings I am expected to attend?
5. What is the philosophy of the university?
6. What are the long-term goals of the university?
7. On what types of committees might I be expected to serve? Will I be chairing these committees?
8. Do you anticipate that I will need to hire new deans in the first few years of my appointment? What is the process like?
9. To what extent does the university collaborate with other higher educational institutions, public schools, state agencies, local businesses, and the community?

10. How is the president's cabinet structured? What will be my role within the cabinet?
11. How is the academic affairs budget developed? Do you anticipate the opportunity to hire more faculty in the near future?
12. What will be my role in working with the BoT? Is there an academic affairs committee, and if so, how often does it meet separately from the board?

In turn, here are questions that may be asked of you:

1. What qualities will you bring to our university if you were to accept this position?
2. What will your strengths be as a provost?
3. What are your weaknesses as a provost?
4. What are your philosophies?
5. What would be your short-/long-term plans if you were to accept this position? Are you interested in someday advancing to a presidency?
6. What has been your experience dealing with budget/personnel cuts or reorganizations?
7. Have you had experience dealing with campus crises? What has been your role in mitigating their effects?
8. Have you helped to start new academic programs? How did you assure their success? Have you been involved in closing academic programs? How did you accomplish it?
9. What has been your experience working with enrollment management (EM) to improve recruitment/retention/graduation rates? What has been your experience working with student affairs on aspects of campus life? Have you been involved in dealing with campus controversies?

Prior to the interview, you should find out as much information as possible about the institution for which you are applying. Much of this information can be gleaned from the institution's website, or provided to you by a recruiting firm if the university is using one. You could use this knowledge during the interview to fulfill several goals, such as to give a clear message to interviewers that you have prepared extremely well for the interview.

This, in turn, demonstrates your interest in and enthusiasm for the position and puts you in a position to show how your leadership is compatible with that of the university. It is always a good idea to learn as much as you can about the academic and employment backgrounds of the people you are likely to meet during the interview—the information will give you insight into their experiences and philosophies and may help you build common ground or avoid pitfalls during the interview.

However, be choosy about when and how you reveal what you know about those you meet—interviewers may be put off to discover that you know a good deal about them, even though the information is public.

When evaluating responses to questions that you pose to their interviewers, you should not only analyze and interpret their verbal responses but collect, analyze, and interpret nonverbal responses exhibited by the interviewers during the course of the interview. It is a good idea toward the end of the interviewing process for you to ask if they need more information about you.

Be assertive in your interview process. Let them know how professional, transparent, and collaborative a leader you are. Present your most important questions to several of the interviewers. This is a good way to ascertain reliability of information. Be cognizant that you are interviewing them to the same extent that they are interviewing you. It is a two-way process. Do not be afraid to ask questions. It is only by asking questions that they can be absolutely sure that you are qualified for the position and that the position is suitable to you.

Particularly if you are from an underrepresented group, you may wish to develop a plan for how you will answer inappropriate or illegal questions about your personal life. It is also possible, in the age of social media, that interviewers will know personal things about you and may ask. Be prepared with a strategy.

CASE 2: A YOUNG MOM CALLED TO BE PROVOST

How does one deal with accepting the position of provost when one is just a young tenured professor with little kids? This is the story of Dr. Lau. Dr. Stevenson, who offered her the job of provost for undergraduate studies, called her to the president's office. She still looks often for the dent in the floor of the president's office where her jaw must have hit it. Dr. Lau had no idea she would be offered such a high-powered position so early in her academic career. She only had a few days to make her decision since the outgoing provost would be around for another week or two and she would need to get up to speed on her work.

After long discussions with her husband, Dr. Lau accepted the job. Immediately, a wide vista of future academic positions opened up. Although many people said that she would make a good university president someday, she focused on the job at hand. Dr. Lau's portfolio included not only undergraduate curriculum and faculty council, but also international initiatives. This made her the university's chief international officer.

During the next two years Dr. Lau worked hard, developed new programs, and tried to break down silos that prevented units from working together. She juggled two kids (ages 5 and 8), ran marathons, attended endless meetings, and traveled monthly for work, all while managing to maintain a semblance of a family life. She faced major challenges in reorganizing the International Office, managing major personnel and personality issues, both at the staff level and in working with other top administrators.

Despite having an extremely supportive spouse, Dr. Lau began to be tired of the monthly travels, attending meetings to discuss issues over which she had little control, and constantly falling behind on her family obligations, leaving most of the raising of her young children to her husband and her mother. Dr. Lau realized at the beginning of her third year as provost that she had reached a crossroads. She could choose a full-time commitment to being an administrator or return to the faculty and have time to devote to her spouse and her kids.

Dr. Lau was torn about what to do. She turned to her mentors. Her former dean, who became a provost at another university, encouraged her to consider stepping out of the administrative track if it was interfering so much with her family life. Her former provost understood the difficulties of juggling her personal life and her administrative career.

When Dr. Lau finally approached the subject with her current boss, the president, he encouraged her to stay, but ultimately understood that she was being pulled in too many directions. Dr. Lau finally came to the realization that administrative jobs would still be there in five years but helping her kids to grow up would not.

Dr. Lau doesn't regret the three years she spent as provost. She has learned more about herself and her abilities than she had at almost any other time in her career. She made wonderful friends, and developed a whole new set of mentors who will continue to be supportive of her over the years. She gained a new respect for university administration, developed a better understanding of the pros and cons of faculty governance, and learned exactly how difficult it is to be a university president.

Most importantly, she has gained a great deal of confidence in herself, and realized that she has many opportunities ahead, whether it is as an academic or as an administrator. Dr. Lau feels fortunate to have had the experience as she counts down the days until her leave starts and can spend quality time with her husband and kids.

Questions

1. Did you accept a position as provost early in your career?
2. Do you agree with Dr. Lau's decision to step down as provost to spend more time with her family?

3. Are administrative jobs like the provost difficult to have while you are raising young kids?
4. Were her mentors right on how they counseled Dr. Lau?

CASE 3: A DEAN PREPARING TO BE A PROVOST

In general, a provost should have a tapestry of skills, knowledge, and wisdom. Dean Nadia thought she was well prepared for this position. As a dean, she had been through a core-curriculum revision, led overseas classes, written grants, worked on outcomes-based teaching and learning assessment, and taught courses with lab sections and without. She experienced dysfunctional committees and ones that did a great job of assessing and solving problems.

Dr. Nadia grew up in an era that encouraged the questioning of authority. Consequently, she found her voice and her understanding of leadership as she held various leadership positions. At her previous institution, she had come to the campus with a one-year appointment and was determined to turn it into a full-time faculty position. She succeeded, becoming the chair of her department, vice president of the senate, director of the faculty center, associate provost, and, finally, an associate dean.

When Dr. Nadia became a dean at another institution, all of a sudden her voice became the dean's voice. She was well respected by her peers, the VPs, and the president on the campus. The many years of academic positions had prepared her well when she thought of taking a provost's job.

Provosts must take responsibility for making hard decisions and communicating them to others. Dr. Nadia had to learn how to do that early in her academic career. She was a junior faculty member on an undergraduate honors committee and needed to make decisions when budget cuts were pressing. As chair, associate provost, and associate dean, she was faced with a myriad of hard decisions. Probably the hardest decision for her was when as a dean she had to eliminate several faculty positions. As she talked with the people in those positions, Dr. Nadia remembered saying to herself, "Well, this is good practice for communicating tough reality."

As dean, Dr. Nadia made some decisions that she regretted. Life is made up of choices required with less information than one desires. They frequently are made in the midst of a series of prior decisions that did not involve the current person in charge. Along the way, Dr. Nadia learned to live with the fact that she can make the best decision only within the context of the issue, the facts available, and the time allowed. Not making a decision, and continuing to mull over options, is generally more destructive than making the decision and moving on. How to deal with risk and uncertainty is a real issue when one is holding a senior administration position.

Dr. Nadia also thought that parenting, especially as a single parent as she was, probably did more to prepare her for the role of dean (and would prepare her for the role of provost), than anything else. Parenting teaches us that we have no control over the personalities of the people we live and interact with, that we have to work with what we are given.

In the face of parental crises, Dr. Nadia had to learn to take one day at a time, without letting her anxiety take over. She used to repeat to herself: *"Don't let your anxiety rise to the level of their anxiety,"* and *"Just because it is their crisis does not mean that it is your crisis."* Keeping calm and centered in the face of chaos had helped her deal with problems on the job like budget cuts, retention challenges, and faculty problems.

Dr. Nadia had also learned administrative lessons from publishing and writing grants. Peer review is always good for developing thick skin and a habit of persistence. Nothing does more for character development than the experience of thinking one's job is done when the manuscript is sent off, only to get reviewers' comments months later, requiring major revisions and resubmission. Publishing and grant writing teaches persistence and resilience. It had developed Dr. Nadia's ability to take criticism without letting it personally wound her and to come back with a better, clearer idea.

Throughout her academic life, lessons about fit came in handy. Thinking about whether one is fitted to a particular institution can be difficult because it involves setting aside one's ego and thinking about what one brings to the table and what other people need. When Dr. Nadia was the dean, she had an "aha" moment while she was attending a Higher Education Resource Services (HERS) seminar. She went through an exercise of assessing her personal leadership style and quickly realized that she had what it takes to be a provost.

But as life continued, she chose to retire before she pursued that goal. This was not about a failure to commit as much as an awareness that she needed to move her life in other directions where she was needed more.

One of the best pieces of advice that Dr. Nadia received on her professional journey to becoming a provost was to always tell the truth. This is different from not telling a lie which is frequently accomplished by omission. Telling the truth requires one to develop an authentic voice, one that speaks from the heart.

Dr. Nadia once accepted an invitation to lecture on sustainability to a difficult audience. Her goal was to speak authentically, and also to engage and "enjoy" those who disagreed with her. Telling the truth, with the goal of effectively engaging an audience in enlightening conversations, leads to stronger relationships and builds on transparency rather than agreement.

As administrators, we cannot control the behavior of others. We can only define boundaries, put incentives in place, and hold people accountable. We can't say everything we want to say at the time we want to say it; we have to pick the right battles and depend on multiple voices to get a message across.

We have to keep our eyes on the future so as to not let the anxiety of the present rule our responses. And we have to like people even if their behavior sometimes drives us crazy.

Questions

1. Do you agree with Dr. Nadia's assessment of leadership preparedness?
2. Do you think that deans make the best provosts?
3. Do you agree that writing papers and grants is a good learning tool to thicken one's skin?
4. Do you agree that parenthood also can prepare us well to be senior administrators?
5. Do you agree with telling the truth and being transparent?

Scenario 1

Dr. Casey was asked by her president to take an interim provost position. After serious consideration, she accepted his offer. Dr. Casey realized that she needed to be keenly aware of the issues currently facing higher education and how these issues impact academic affairs. She also realized that the position required the skill of multitasking and flexibility. That is, informed, collaborative decision-making and an ability to make the tough calls while not losing her humanity, empathy, and civility.

For Dr. Casey, working her way through the academic landscape as a professor and administrator at the unit level, and then at the institutional level, provided the necessary skill set to understand the job from multiple perspectives. Additionally, the opportunities she was afforded to visit many college campuses in her role as an accreditation evaluator broadened her knowledge of how this role functions on a college campus.

Because Dr. Casey had been at the institution for several years in different capacities, she felt comfortable with the campus and the individuals with whom she was expected to interact. Dr. Casey was promised, and received strong support from the president, and from fellow cabinet members. The timing for the position was not the best as she had recently adopted a toddler. Initially, family chipped in with childcare and the entire campus community became her child's extended family. The position, however, certainly did demand long days, evenings, and weekend responsibilities, which presented a huge challenge for Dr. Casey.

Scenario 2

After being a dean for many years, Dr. Vivaan applied for a provost position. He knew he would be responsible to the president but he didn't know exactly how much freedom he would have to do the many things he wanted to do for academic affairs. Dr. Vivaan thought he was prepared because he had been a good dean for many years and watched carefully what was happening on his campus. He recognized things he wanted to do differently than the provost he was working for.

Dr. Vivaan started preparing for the search and interview process. He researched the place he was applying thoroughly and also knew from experience how to be aware of clues during the interviewing process.

The university he was applying to had a search firm for the position. Dr. Vivaan trusted that they will be giving him the best advice, but realized that they were working for the university, not working for him. One of his mentors recommended that he get a coach to help him prepare for the interview. The coach suggested reading everything about the university, in particular the strategic plan and the master plan.

During the interview process Dr. Vivaan fell in love with the place and immediately knew it was "the right fit" for him. He also knew that accepting the job was going to affect his personal and family life, since he was moving to another state and his wife had a great academic job where they lived.

Dr. Vivaan was lucky in that his wife was very understanding and she commuted every weekend to see him, and his daughters were grown and out of the house. He knew he could not have done this when his kids where young. Not being with his wife during the week didn't matter much to him since he was so busy with many events almost every evening. Dr. Vivaan truly enjoyed his years as provost and he felt he made the right decision accepting the job.

Scenario 3

Dr. Zane was a dean at a comprehensive university contemplating a transition to a provost position. The best preparation she had for becoming a provost was time spent reviewing tenure and promotion cases with the other school deans and the provost at her institution. Dr. Zane is a scientist, so she had little trouble reading cases from the science, technology, engineering and math (STEM) disciplines. The dean in the nursing school taught her about the health professions, which made Dr. Zane comfortable with those disciplines.

But it was sitting with the dean of the School of Humanities and Arts, and the provost who came from the School of Education, that helped her learn what scholarship and teaching look like in disciplines that were very different from hers, and in turn they learned from Dr. Zane about STEM disciplines.

Learning about all different disciplines in the academy gave Dr. Zane enough confidence to support faculty in disciplines far from her own, and to question things in tenure and promotion cases that did not seem to apply to those disciplines. She also learned a great deal about the facilities, curricula, and advising needs of those areas. She felt that she was well qualified to take a provost position when she applied for one.

Scenario 4

Dr. Readable was a historian when he became a provost at a small private university. One of his main challenges were the STEM disciplines in his university. He knew he needed to learn about life/health/safety issues, the equipment issues, and the Institutional Animal Care and Use Committee (IACUC) and Institutional Research Board (IRB) regulatory issues that come with overseeing programs in these areas. He also needed to learn about the safety issues in theater, studio art, and the IRB issues in the School of Business and the School of Education.

In preparation, he took time to tour lab spaces and ask questions about the committees and officers who managed these issues. He took a crash course on how to dispose of hazardous waste, radioactive waste, and medical waste, about protocols for reviewing research proposals according to federal guidelines, and about grant processes. This was important to him because he knew that these areas were crucial for teaching and faculty research in the STEM disciplines and a lapse in these areas was very serious.

As provost, he knew he was the person that would "go to jail" in the event of a serious issue. His good friend, a dean of science at a public institution known as ILU, shared the following story with Dr. Readable. The biology department at ILU had been growing in animal research. However, when the dean asked the chair of the biology department which faculty member chaired the IACUC, the chair gave him a blank look and asked, "What's an IACUC?"

The dean ended up taking a group of faculty to a three-day "IACUC 101" meeting and setting up an IACUC to make sure that the university complied with regulations and were eligible to receive federal research funding. Provost Readable understood he needed to ask questions about laboratory safety as he discovered problems, such as failure to dispose of old chemicals in a safe and timely manner, art studios with no ventilation which exposed students to hazardous fumes, and fume hoods not functioning or improperly vented.

Provost Readable wanted to be sure he knew the risks, and was prepared to spend money to remediate problem areas. As his friend, the dean at ILU, told him, "Lives depend on it."

Scenario 5

Provost Ramadashan read many reports before taking the position of provost at a comprehensive university. He had read that 86 percent of American colleges and universities think the academic health of their institutions is quite strong. Twelve percent think their institutions' academic health is fair, and only one percent said it was poor or failing. But while Provost Ramadashan understood that those finding might suggest provosts are feeling confident about how their institutions are fulfilling their many missions, he knew that was probably not quite the case and that provosts are more critical.

When it comes to many of the larger challenges that provosts face, he knew from talking to friends that they aren't always so confident. Provost Ramadashan's institution was facing pressure to hire more minority faculty members and he was uncertain about how he would be able to meet targets for diversifying his faculty. At the same time, the senate was reviewing the curriculum and requiring at least one course in a diversity-related topic for all undergraduates.

Provost Ramadashan read a report that had intensified the perception that in the last year, student evaluations of faculty members' teaching reflected bias against female and minority professors. Provost Ramadashan wanted to understand the context of those evaluations before considering changes in process. Provost Ramadashan had also read multiple articles about assessment and he was confident about implementing processes for improvements in teaching and learning.

FINAL THOUGHTS

Before you are a leader, success is all about growing yourself. When you become a leader, success is all about growing others.

—Jack Welch

Although the process of applying for senior academic-leadership positions is painful and tedious, it's worth it. Remember to study the university to which you are applying. Institutions and departments want to feel that you have some special affinity for them.

Make sure your application materials answer that big "why us?" question. Read the hiring criteria. Pay attention to the search consultant's advice on local areas of pride, ambition, or worry. Familiarize yourself with the institution's strategic plan. Identify major ideas or aspirations. Try to find statements or speeches given by the senior administrators who will be hiring you. Check out the bios of the search committee members to take the pulse of who your immediate audience will be.

Your cover letter is much more important than your curriculum vitae. Search firms sometimes discourage committees from requiring a cover letter early in the search. Apparently there are some candidates who hesitate to enter a pool because of the time commitment of writing the letter when they are not sure they are even likely to be considered. We advise you to submit one regardless of whether it is required. The effort to do so makes a positive impression on committees and will help you focus on whether this is really an opportunity you want to pursue.

Be sure to reflect the key job requirements listed in the hiring profile. Cite experiences and accomplishments that demonstrate your relevant talents. Be positive, be charismatic, and be assured of yourself. And don't forget to smile; smiles go a long way.

Chapter 2

Arriving on Campus

"The Honeymoon Period"

This chapter focuses on learning the campus culture of a new institution and how the first steps can help or hinder cohesive relationships across the campus. It includes personal stories and cases on how provosts have used the "honeymoon period" to set up strategies for change and directions for the academic division.

When a new provost is hired from outside the institution, the new arrival is usually welcomed with open arms and with high hopes by all the relevant campus constituencies. Competing campus groups share a desire for the success of the new provost and are eager to help the provost learn the history, culture, governance, and politics of the university.

On that first, sunnily optimistic day, the new provost has made no difficult decisions and has alienated no campus opinion leaders. While the next crisis and the university culture will determine how long this honeymoon period will last, honeymoons generally last for at least a few months and may last for as long as the first year.

Most new provosts see the honeymoon period as the opportunity to learn as much as they can about their new institution and their work in it, including the formal governance structure, its leading formal and informal influencers (e.g., trustees, prominent faculty), and its deep culture. Provosts have multiple bosses, of course, in the form of trustees and presidents, and the provosts of public universities also may have required interactions with legislators and gubernatorial employees and appointees.

The honeymoon period additionally offers the new provost some opportunity to shape an informed agenda for effective management and leadership, subject to constraints imposed from above and the limiting factors of students, physical plant, employees, money, and history.

Most provosts find that the honeymoon does not survive the first major crisis or challenge a new provost has to confront, so new provosts can't depend on their honeymoons lasting for any specific duration. Ideally, a new provost, in consultation with the president and various stakeholders, will shape an agenda and begin to implement elements of it within the first few months after taking the position, while there is ample goodwill and there is time to establish a relationship as a proactive leader.

However, another perspective is that new provosts should "ease into" their position, learn the culture, and build trust and identify allies before making ambitious decisions or announcements. From this perspective, a new provost must build capital, and, especially, build relationships, before trying to change the organization. Which of these two strategies will be most effective depends in part on the "health" of the institution (are there ongoing crises or are operations relatively stable?) and on the institution's appetite for change (are other members of the leadership team relatively new, or is the new provost joining a well-established group?).

The honeymoon period, with its many advantages, represents the new provost's most fundamental problem: sooner or later, different constituencies will want different things from the same provost. Trustees may want revisions to campus governance and the creation of new academic programs. Faculty may want their own revisions in shared governance, possibly in ways at odds with trustee priorities, along with more investment in traditional programs the trustees treat with skepticism.

Deans and chairs may want more decision-making autonomy, with the suggestion that the new provost give up some of the power (and money) associated with the provost's office. Presidents may want provosts to enact presidential priorities not shared by their provosts.

At a time when many universities are competing for fewer prospective students and coping with cuts in public funding, there are few institutions today that leave new provosts alone to learn for six to twelve months about the existing management and leadership structure of the university. For better or worse, the new provost must learn and lead at the same time, relying on her or his reservoir of experience and capacity for good judgment to get through the early days of the new job.

BUILDING RELATIONSHIPS
DURING THE HONEYMOON

When a provost is truly new to the institution, he or she must establish relationships at every turn. Which subordinates are especially suited to becoming regular sources of guidance and good advice? Which academic leaders have reputations for looking out primarily for their own interests?

To make the best use of the honeymoon period, new provosts should seriously consider the creation of a transition plan, with goals for that plan (especially in the first ninety days) and a systematic scheme for meeting and developing relationships with leaders from every major constituent group. Such transition plans ordinarily include ways to spend time and to build relationships with multiple representatives from many or all of the following groups:

- Trustees
- President
- President's office staff
- Vice presidents and others reporting directly to the president
- Deans
- Associate provosts, associate vice presidents, and other direct reports
- Department chairs and program directors
- Directors of academic support offices
- Full-time and part-time faculty
- Academic affairs staff
- Relevant staff outside academic affairs (e.g., Human Resources)
- Donors
- Alumni
- Local and state politicians
- Neighborhood association leaders

While trustees at many universities will organize a formal transition committee and prepare a written transition plan for a new president, new provosts are usually on their own when putting together such plans. The new provost cannot put together a transition plan without very significant assistance, however, as the new provost can only guess, for example how important it is to meet with one donor before another and how important the provost's relationship will be with the general counsel.

Whoever is on the list to meet with the new provost in those early weeks, the provost is trying to understand the people, the personalities, and (perhaps most importantly) the campus culture. While the transition plan need not be an elaborate written document, we do not recommend that new provosts "wing it" in their opening weeks on the job.

STEPS TO TAKE TO LEARN YOUR CAMPUS CULTURE

Learning the campus culture of a new institution will play a big role in how the new provost is perceived by other institutional colleagues, as well as those you supervise. Understanding the influence of the campus culture is never a simple matter, because culture, even within a single institution, is heterogeneous and dynamic. To add to the complexity, people pay attention to different things in their environment and may understand the same experiences differently. For that reason, many aspects of campus culture will have different meanings and relevance for different people.

You need to reach out to many constituencies. Listen, observe, and read documents, but many times the most powerful messengers of your campus culture are your own students. Give your students a platform to speak to what it's like to be enrolled in your college or university.

A colleague of ours always says to rely on a good sense of humor. You know you've got what it takes to be the provost. They hired you over the other candidates, whether internal or external. Now you need to show that you can do the job. A sense of humor is key to impressing the people you work with that you are a positive person. Understanding the campus culture will allow you to use the sense of humor in areas that your colleagues will appreciate.

Also, don't be afraid of showing your uniqueness and how this amazing "you" fits with the campus culture. Determine what you can provide to your new institution that no one else can. Determine how you can improve your new university to make its reputation the best in your region.

WHEN THERE IS NO HONEYMOON

As mentioned earlier, any new provost is likely to have a honeymoon period, ranging from a few weeks in the worst case to several months in the best-case scenario. Some provosts, however, will not have much a honeymoon period, or will have none at all.

First, interim provosts are sometimes appointed after a provost leaves abruptly. In such cases, interim provosts may have only a few days or weeks to prepare for their new position. For example, one of the coauthors of this book was appointed as an interim provost about forty-eight hours before beginning in the position. In such cases, there is little time to build goodwill or to create the conditions for even a brief honeymoon period.

Second, it is not uncommon for interim provosts or internal candidates to become permanent provosts. These internal candidates presumably are known quantities and proven leaders with a deep understanding of the university and already-existing alliances and networks that can be used to facilitate work on difficult tasks. One of the disadvantages of any internal candidate who becomes provost, though, is the likelihood that the new provost will not have a honeymoon.

After all, many of the same attributes that made the internal candidate attractive will prevent any honeymoon period. The new provost needs few or no introductions. Importantly, the new provost is perceived as a known quantity and may be given little chance to set a new tone or to make a new impression. If the new provost has previously been in a position of authority, the new provost may also have disappointed some individuals or groups as a result of decisions made months or years earlier. Put bluntly, the internal candidate will likely have detractors before beginning the first day of work as a provost.

Third, some new provosts take office in the middle of a crisis, and the usual work of a transition period may be set aside because of the exigencies of the moment. A provost who starts work a week into the efforts of the adjunct faculty to unionize, or two weeks before a very public sexual harassment claim is made against a well-known dean, will likely have to forgo any hopes for a meaningful honeymoon period.

RECOMMENDATIONS FROM A SEASONED PROVOST

Dr. Ng has been a provost at his institution for fifteen years. He hopes that his advice can be helpful to new provosts embarking on their administrative journeys, helping them avoid some of the pitfalls that can often derail a successful tenure as a chief academic officer. His first advice is to be wary of those individuals who are the first to make an appointment with you and be sure you research the history of any initial request (for anything) you receive. Resist the temptation to demonstrate that you are a "strong leader" by making big decisions too soon. Think of yourself as "institutional gravity," stable and centered, and after a long day, go home.

The world of higher education has certainly changed in the past five years, and the challenges of effectively leading an academic program have increased many times over. The financial situation during the last five years has left many provosts wondering about the future of their institutions. Words and phrases like "unsustainable," "rising discount rates and declining net tuition revenue," "structural budget deficits," and "restructuring" have become common elements of the higher administration vernacular.

Votes of no confidence have increasingly dotted the landscape of higher education as faculty express their frustration with financial constraints and the lack of momentum or shared vision for their institutions. In short, the job of the provost, which many claim to be the most difficult in higher education, has become even more difficult. So, if you have just accepted a provost position and are trying to do your best to lead in difficult times, please consider a few of Dr. Ng's observations based on his experience.

Read any prospectus for a presidential or provost position and you will find the term "shared governance." While the concept of shared governance has always been an essential element of any college campus, years of budget reductions and shaky financial footing have brought about even greater interest on the part of faculty, staff, and students in the decision-making processes. Finding ways to engage the campus community in shared governance is important and necessary, but it does have its challenges.

You should always remember that shared governance does not mean shared accountability. In the academic sphere, the accountability is all yours, no matter how shared the decision-making process was. And it is rare that a system of shared governance will consistently yield results that are satisfactory to everyone. Shared governance is essential—but not perfect. If your campus has a faculty union, it is also essential that you know the relationship between the union and the "shared governance" structure of your institution.

At some, the union will have subsumed the governance process. At others, the two will remain distinct but have some overlap—which can often lead to the leadership of the two structures disagreeing with one another. Be sure to find out what your role is, what the history is, and be aware of how you can make both of these areas work in your favor.

Particularly if you are becoming a provost at a small campus, you may find that there has been a tradition of close personal relationships between previous provosts (or deans, or whatever) and members of the faculty (whom they have known for many years). Be very careful. If you have relocated to a new area to join this community, you may be lonely, and it may be tempting to begin to socialize with the tight-knit community you have joined.

While it may be flattering to be invited to the homes of faculty or other administrators, it is also quite possible that such invitations will have political motivations and will be perceived poorly by those around you. Until you have a better idea of the political lay of the land, it may be better to stick to lunches in the faculty dining room or student cafeteria.

Transparency is a very important concept in higher education today. It is important for you to be transparent in your decision-making processes and to demonstrate that you are able to communicate the reasons for your decisions effectively. You should always be willing and able to share with the campus community the information that is shaping the difficult decisions you are making. Keep in mind, however, that transparency can become a challenge when you start to show people things they don't necessarily want to see.

For many provosts who thought the financial challenges were "cyclical" rather than "structural," they probably shielded their faculty, staff, and students from the cold, hard facts, thinking that surely things were going to get better on their own. For those provosts at institutions facing the need for dramatic change, sharing that information for the first time can be a bit sobering, and not always pleasant.

You should know that clear and consistent communication is an essential element of effective leadership, yet you may find that people will question your ability as a communicator. Keep in mind that the difference between effective communication and ineffective communication occasionally has nothing to do with actual process, but more with the content of the message.

When people are hearing the things they want to hear, it is often the case that they will perceive the communication to be effective. But, when they are hearing things they don't want to hear, they may perceive the communication to be ineffective, even if the communication process is excellent. So, always strive to communicate effectively, but be prepared to hear that you haven't. If this happens, just be patient and try again.

Eventually, the message will get through. As you prepare to communicate on major issues or difficult issues, you will need to be sure that your president and possibly others on the board (and in senior leadership) are in agreement with your communication plan. You will need to make sure that others in leadership will back you up, and that they will refer faculty who may try to go around your back to you. If your campus has a communications director, you may even be able to work with that person to devise the best strategies.

There is chance that you may feel a bit underappreciated. You may feel that the good work you do goes unnoticed and positive feedback is in limited supply. You may have reached the point of asking yourself whether doing good work is even worth the effort. The answer, of course, is that it is indeed worth the effort and there are two reasons why.

First, it is your job to do good work. You have a responsibility and a commitment to your institution to give your best effort, all of the time. Second, and perhaps more importantly, doing good work makes you feel better about yourself and the work you are doing. Knowing that you have done your job well, whatever the project or challenge might be, will lift your spirits and bolster your confidence more than anything else you can do, even if it goes unnoticed or is unappreciated.

You have just been hired, but over the past five years, it is likely that your institution has experienced some form of turmoil. Perhaps there has been a vote of no confidence in the administration or announcements of budget cuts and layoffs, or both. There may be student demonstrations, there may be high-profile cases of faculty or administrators behaving badly, and there may be a strike by a faculty or graduate student union. When events like this occur, they can create chaos within a campus community that make life challenging for everyone.

Schisms between faculty and the administration or between faculty and staff or even between faculty and faculty are likely to emerge. Factions and alliances are formed and trust is destroyed. Human beings cannot tolerate chaos for long periods of time and will slowly begin to gravitate toward sanity and calm. You need to be one of those sane and calm people.

Students are the reason our institutions exist, and you need to spend as much time as you can with them. If you have not found a way to teach a class, as Dr. Ng had the privilege of doing in his time as provost, you need to find a way to make that happen. Spending time in the classroom with your students is the best way to recognize the importance of your work, and keep the challenges that go along with it in the proper perspective. Those hours that you spend with your students will refocus and energize you.

Dr. Ng has also found that playing an active role in academic advising has a similar effect. But, if you can't do those things, do what you can. Go to a student presentation or sit and talk with students in the cafeteria. Anything that you can do to connect with your students is sure to remind you of why you wanted to become a university administrator; to play a key role in transforming the lives and minds of your students.

Scenario 1

Dr. Abda-Alim was appointed by her president as an interim provost. She knew that she needed to quickly learn the campus culture from a perspective of an administrator and not a faculty member. Dr. Abda-Alim decided to meet individually and in groups with all of the various constituencies, often on their "turf." Luckily, given that she had many years of experience at her institution, it wasn't so much getting to know the campus culture, but adjusting to her new role in this culture.

Dr. Abda-Alim believed she was appointed to help further the president's agenda and vision (with which she agreed), and because it was known that she was not a candidate for the permanent position, she was free to act without worrying about what was best for "her" as opposed to what was best for the institution. This was true even at the risk of it being an unpopular decision, so she did what was necessary to support the president.

Dr. Abda-Alim learned a lot, and was able to have the support of many colleagues. She enjoyed her two years as interim provost and was able to accomplish many things, among them a five-year strategic plan, a master plan, and the creation of new programs.

Scenario 2

After many years of successful service as a dean and associate provost at a comprehensive teaching university, Dr. Mohamed applied for a provost's position at a selective liberal arts college in a neighboring state. After a very pleasant round of interviews, Dr. Mohamed was announced with great fanfare as the new provost and began planning the move to his new institution. A few days after the announcement, Dr. Mohamed receives a letter, signed by about a third of the tenured faculty at the liberal arts college.

The letter indicates that he did not receive the support of the majority of the faculty in an advisory vote that was reported to the president. The letter suggests that Dr. Mohamed was opposed by many faculty because his employment history, academic discipline, and doctorate in education did not seem sufficiently prestigious to most of the faculty, though a minority of faculty had supported him because of his strong administrative record.

The letter politely requests that he withdraw from the position. When asked about the faculty letter, the president of the liberal arts college acknowledges that the letter is accurate and reiterates her strong support for Dr. Mohamed. The president assures him that the faculty will get over their concerns once they get to know him. Dr. Mohamed notified the liberal arts college that he would like to rescind his acceptance of the offer.

While he understood that universal faculty support for any one candidate following an open national search is unlikely, he concluded that he could not trust a president who did not fully and truthfully describe the faculty objections when the job was initially offered. After another year as associate provost at his current institution, he accepted another provostship.

WORKING WITH UNIONS

CASE 1: A PROVOST'S REACTION TO THE FORMATION OF A FACULTY UNION

Provost Johnson is a fairly new provost at a small Historically Black Colleges and Universities (HCBU) campus. The faculty, which is not unionized, is having a secret ballot election to determine if union representation is wanted.

The provost fears that the creation of a faculty union may significantly alter the collegial relationship that he enjoys with his faculty and may impede, rather than facilitate, the continuous progress that he is making to uplift and improve the university.

The introduction of a union would, according to the provost, present a barrier to effective communication with the faculty—a privilege that he appreciates and values, and from which the entire academic community benefits. Electing a union to be the representative of the faculty means that the university (the president and the provost) may not deal directly with the faculty concerning wages, hours, and terms and conditions of employment. Instead, the university will have to deal with the union representatives.

Provost Johnson's experience has been that unions are usually less interested in negotiating on behalf of individuals based on their contributions, talents, and accomplishments, and more interested in negotiating on behalf of the group.

Prior to the vote, the provost encourages the faculty to obtain sufficient information to determine whether this union will fairly represent the faculty, whether it has a record of success in representing similar constituencies, and how much money it will cost members to be represented by the union. The provost asks the faculty whether union representation at the university will be an investment that will advance the faculty interests, or an additional monetary expense without commensurate benefit, which would lower the net faculty pay.

For the provost, these are essential questions and he works to share information with the faculty that facilitates their due diligence.

The provost has gathered data and based on university discussions, only a minority of nontenure track full-time faculty have signed "authorization cards" seeking union representation. No tenured faculty have joined this effort. That suggests to Provost Johnson that many of the faculty may not be aware of the interest in union representation.

Despite the union's apparent appeal to only a minority, it is extremely important that all eligible voters cast a ballot in the election. The reason for this is because the election outcome is determined by a majority of the votes actually cast, not a majority of the eligible voters. So the provost urges all faculty to become fully informed about this critical issue and to participate in the election. He even posts a Q&A website and holds several forums with the faculty.

Voting day comes and a large majority rejects union representation. Provost Johnson is happy and proud of his performance during this time.

Questions

1. How would you handle a situation like that faced by Provost Johnson?
2. Do you consider a unionized campus an impediment or a benefit?
3. How much do you know about unions in academic settings?
4. Where would you turn for information?
5. Do you agree with Provost Johnson's approach to his faculty before the vote?

CASE 2: A "UNION" PROVOST GOES NONUNION

Provost Popkin had spent much of his career as a faculty member and as a dean at unionized campuses. While he appreciated the protections the union had provided him as a faculty member, particularly prior to tenure, as a dean he had found working with the faculty union frustrating. Misbehaving faculty were allowed to remain in the classroom pending union grievance processes and changes to faculty workload that would improve university quality were stalled for years by a combination of shared governance and union maneuvering.

Provost Popkin often felt that students were the ultimate losers in these situations, so he looked forward to becoming the provost at the College of Cumberland, which had no faculty union. He was sure he'd have an easier time implementing important changes there.

On arriving, however, Provost Popkin was disturbed to discover many irregularities that had never been a problem at his previous campus. First, there were many faculty who enjoyed greatly reduced workloads or special stipends—many of which appeared to be simply largesse from a previous provost in return for some past political favor. Few of these were supported by documentation, but a coalition of favored faculty threatened to stall Popkin's initiatives if their special arrangements were altered.

Second, Popkin discovered that there were irregularities in faculty salaries that seemed biased against female and minority faculty, but the CFO resisted the idea of simply raising salaries of the affected faculty to create greater equity. Then, Popkin was confronted by a group of faculty who claimed to have evidence of gross negligence on the part of one of their colleagues, but the claims went back years and there was no documentation in the provost's office.

Instead of leading change, Popkin felt he spent most of his time trying to untangle these messy faculty problems without causing a faculty revolt. He realized that many of these problems would not have occurred, or would have been dealt with systematically, at the unionized campuses where he had previously served.

Questions

1. If you work on a unionized campus now, how has the union been helpful to the campus? Do you believe it has harmed the campus?
2. How might Popkin's problems have been addressed had a faculty union been in place at the College of Cumberland?
3. In the absence of a union, how might Popkin be able to address the biases and inequities in a transparent manner?

CASE 3: UNION VERSUS GOVERNANCE

Ocean University (OU) serves a largely working-class population on the outskirts of a major metropolitan area. Formed decades ago from a merger between two smaller colleges (Peninsula College and Promontory College), it now boasts both robust two-year career-focused programs and strong four-year liberal arts and professional degree programs. OU has both a strong faculty union and a strong tradition of shared governance, both of which date back to days before the merger.

Provost Ahmedi, eager to get off to a good start with both union and governance bodies, invited the president of the union chapter and the chair of the Faculty Senate to a lunch meeting just a few days after she began her work at OU. She chose the faculty dining room as the venue, hoping that many faculty would see the three of them together and understand that she wanted to work well with both groups.

Unfortunately, the lunch did not go as she expected. As Provost Ahmedi laid out her agenda, she found that the two faculty leaders disagreed with one another on every point—if the union president liked an item, the senate chair hated it, and vice versa. At times, the conversation got heated, and pretty soon Ahmedi noticed that faculty around the dining room were staring at their table in ways that made her wish they were dining elsewhere.

The next day Ahmedi had a visit from a very senior faculty member, a former dean, who had witnessed the debacle in the dining room. He pointed out to her that if she perused a list of those faculty who had been leaders or officers in the union, nearly all of them came from Peninsula College—which had been the birthplace of most of the two-year degree programs. Those faculty who served as senators most always came originally from Promontory College and had developed the four-year programs.

The former dean suggested that Ahmedi take a close look at the CVs of the faculty involved. When she did, she discovered that the faculty who had formerly been at Promontory had much more extensive publication records than those from Peninsula, who had often taught more and larger classes before the merger. She realized that the two power structures around the faculty actually represented two different cultural and historical traditions at OU, and that she would need to consider ways in which, over time, she could forge a new culture that respected both traditions.

Questions

1. How should Provost Ahmedi approach the issue of multiple faculty cultures on campus?
2. How might conflict between union leadership and governance leadership harm, or help, Provost Ahmedi's agenda?
3. Can a solution be found?

CASE 4: THE NEW PROVOST AND THE
STRONG UNION PRESIDENT

Dr. Young was the successful provost candidate at a small, unionized college. Before becoming provost, her administrative experience was on non-unionized campuses. The union president has had significant power at this college for many years. The current and past presidents have bowed to the union leader who has successfully negotiated very powerful contracts for the faculty. After Provost Young joins the campus, the union president quickly makes sure that the new provost understands that he will continue to rule and that she will have no authority within academic affairs.

Unfortunately, the college is in serious financial difficulty. A new faculty contract will be negotiated during the coming summer and the administration feels that a better contract is necessary to improve the fiscal situation. Provost Young will be presiding over the negotiations along with the college counsel.

In preparation for the negotiations, Provost Young paid close attention to the current union contract and asked the college counsel to walk her through the nuances of the agreement. The provost studied the current policies and procedures, and started working on a plan to develop a collaborative and transparent process to change those policies that were an impediment to the mission and strategic plan of the college. In particular, she knew she must focus on those that contributed to the current financial problems.

The union president was known for his devious strategies and manipulative personality, traits the provost quickly understood given her initial exposure to him. Consequently, she was very careful not to engage in unfruitful conversations with him or let herself be drawn into negotiations prematurely.

In the month prior to the start of negotiations, Provost Young asked permission from the president to hire a contract lawyer from a highly recommended firm. She also put together a contract committee that included deans, chairs, faculty members, and the VP of finance. After significant deliberation, the committee developed a plan to increase revenue for the institution while preserving some of the faculty perks that existed.

Negotiation starts and the union president refuses to read the provost's proposal, threatening to leave the negotiation table. He has used this tactic in prior negotiations, as well as threatening faculty strikes. The president is very worried about a strike, but the provost reassures him that the contract lawyer she just hired will be able to maneuver the negotiations and come to an agreement with the union president.

After months of negotiation, Provost Young, with the help of the lawyer and the university counsel, is able to reach a consensus, reclaiming some parts of the contract that will help the institution to develop a better fiscal base. At the same time, she is able to reassure the faculty that once the institution is financially stable, they will reopen negotiations on some "hot" topics. The union president is livid. For the first time in thirty years, he had lost control of a contract negotiation. The university president congratulates Provost Young for her performance and the vision to hire an external contract lawyer.

Provost Young recognized that she learned a lot about contact negotiations during the process and realizes it was a worthwhile experience. However, she is not looking forward to repeating it in five years and recognizes how important it was to have a capable contract law expert at the table.

Questions

1. Do you agree with the way Provost Young handled the situation?
2. Have you ever been an administrator on a campus with a faculty union?
3. How will you prepare for contract negotiations if you are part of the negotiation team?
4. How do you balance union power when faced with fiscal restraints at institutions that are financially strained?

CASE 5: DRESS FOR SUCCESS— MANY SMALL STORIES

A. Dean Arroyo was searching for a provost position and had an opportunity to be part of a group that did mock interviews with search consultants who advised candidates on how to present themselves best for the next stage of their careers. He got a fresh haircut and chose his suit, shoes, and tie carefully, to be fairly conservative but also interesting. During his presentation to the panel of consultants, one consultant commented, "You should not choose a brown tie—it matches and emphasizes your skin color."

B. Provost Lester had a good deal of experience interacting with the BoT at her previous position, so she felt confident as she prepared for her first board meeting at Central University. She chose a very sharp skirt suit, which others had praised whenever she wore it—the fabric was a jewel tone that flattered her eye color. During a break between sessions the female chair of the finance committee greeted Provost Lester and commented, "I remember when I first served on a corporate board, I also made the mistake of wearing a bright color to a board meeting."

C. Provost Alameda had served for nearly a decade at Upper Middle State University, where she was the first woman to hold the position and had some notable successes to her credit. She was happy when a leadership organization asked her to present at a workshop for women in higher education. At the workshop, some of the women in attendance expressed surprise that Provost Alameda wore elaborate earrings that dangled—many of them had been warned, or even chastised about, wearing "obtrusive" jewelry on the job. Provost Alameda laughed gently at their comments and replied, "Oh yes, I've been told that too . . . but I love earrings like this and I refuse to give them up."

Questions

1. Do you think that provosts should have a "personal style" in how they present themselves, or should provosts strive to blend in with campus norms for appearance?
2. How would you respond during an interview, a board meeting, or a cabinet meeting if someone criticized your appearance?
3. Do you add your voice to group conversations after a member has criticized someone else's appearance apparently out of prejudice? What might you say?

FINAL THOUGHTS

To be persuasive we must be believable; to be believable we must be credible; to be credible we must be truthful.

—Edward R. Murrow

Honeymoon periods are not long, so take advantage of what you have. Ideally, you will be granted a grace period to begin enacting your promised agenda before they start doubting your leadership. In practice, you may encounter roadblocks that will end your honeymoon much sooner than you expected. Your first step should be a reconnaissance mission to determine if any crises demand big decisions right away. Use your time wisely to learn, gain trust, get to know people, let them size you up, build consensus, and assign priorities.

If you are facing budget cuts, accept that your honeymoon is going to be short because "every dollar has a constituency." Use your first months to listen, never preach. Remember that people will question your motives in every step until they get to know you better. Use this honeymoon period to meet with everyone you can, individually or in small groups. Hear people out, ponder, consider, ask follow-up questions, connect dots, and map patterns. Explore your new world and its citizens and try to show that you want the best for all of them.

In your first few months on the job, make decisions on some easy issues while planning for the difficult ones (as the phrase goes "look for the low hanging fruit"). Hindsight makes us feel wise. Faculty and staff members may tempt you to lambaste the previous regime. Don't join in the booing. First, you don't know enough about the place yet to distinguish whether past decisions were the wrong ones and every decision that administrators make involves trade-offs. There is no such thing as a perfect resolution.

Second, the past and the present are not necessarily comparable. Third, after you are gone, people will complain about you to your successor. Your honeymoon should be a positive interval; don't let it get bogged down in recriminations. Most people on any campus want to give the new leader a chance, but nobody gets a free pass forever.

Long or short, your honeymoon is a key period to get settled in, gain wisdom, and set a course for the successful tenure you hope will ensue. The key factor is that even if you are viewed favorably, you are under scrutiny, especially if you are an outsider. Now, in your first months, is the time to establish your credentials as a partner in progress.

Chapter 3

Leading through Diverse Lenses

This chapter addresses the challenges and opportunities presented when a new provost is identifiable as part of an underrepresented group. Being the first provost from a group that has not traditionally been represented (gender, sexuality, race, ethnicity, or even academic discipline) at an institution creates challenges. Overt discrimination, unrealistic expectations, patterns of bias, or previously unmet needs may present significant problems. This chapter provides stories and cases of how provosts in such situations have managed these competing forces.

INTRODUCTION

Provosts are now universally expected to engage the diversity climates at their institutions. Strong application letters for provost positions invariably include some description of the applicant's success in creating more diverse and inclusive campus environments. Finalists for the provost positions always talk about, and are asked to comment on, their approach to supporting diverse campus constituencies. Presidents and governing boards will frequently expect provosts to take a leading role, and sometimes the leading role, on the diversity goals in the university's strategic plan.

The specific diversity interests of a university may vary from one institution to the next. At one university, a recent campus hate-speech or racist comment on social media may weigh heavily and lead to calls for changes in institutional policy or diversity training. At another university, failure to make progress over time on diversifying the faculty or the student body may be the primary source of conversation and concern.

New provosts who are identifiable as part of an underrepresented group may find themselves exposed to the overt problems of discrimination or balancing unrealistic expectations from a group that feels empowered by their appointment. They may unearth patterns of bias or unmet needs that have been unaddressed by previous administrations. At the same time, the symbolic significance of their appointment may create opportunities for leadership that can have a profound positive impact on the institution.

Provosts, and especially new provosts, may find that diversity priorities have shifted over time or are notably different from one university to another. A majority-minority urban university where over 90 percent of faculty identify as white will have very different diversity interests than a rural university where the diversity of the student body has declined over the past five years and where fewer than 5 percent of students are African American, for example.

Shifts in the religious affiliations of students over time may have significant implications for the understanding of diversity on campus, as might the growth in the numbers of students, faculty, and staff who publicly identify as members of the LGBTQ+ community.

While all provosts will be expected to comment regularly on and commit time and resources to meeting institutional diversity goals, the experiences of provosts who are identified as heterosexual white men may be notably different from provosts who are understood as contributing to the diversity of campus leadership. In this chapter, we focus in particular on the experience of provosts who are somehow identified as contributing to the diversity of their university communities.

CASE 1: HOW A MINORITY PROVOST
FELT ABOUT LEAVING THE JOB

Dr. Hand was the first African American hired in an upper administrative job at her university. That was a huge accomplishment for her and improved the diversity of the upper administration, all of whom had been white men. Dr. Hand knew that she had a big responsibility as a role model for her African American faculty and for other provosts that find themselves as minority "tokens" on their campus.

As provost, Dr. Hand had a great many obligations, including responsibility for international programs. When she started the job, Dr. Hand thought that she could make a significant impact on international programs, given her research agenda and her passion for internationalization. As time passed, she could only watch as this favorite part of her portfolio fell from a top priority during her first year as provost, to not being mentioned in the university's capital campaign that launched two years later.

Dr. Hand began to find herself thinking seriously about what she wanted to do, and whether or not she would continue as the provost. At first, this was practically unthinkable, since she was the only African American in a top-level position. And Dr. Hand had done so much for diversifying the culture of her school.

She helped to bring the president to the table when the Center for African and African American studies was having difficulties working with other departments to recruit faculty. When discussing her doubts with a few close colleagues, they would point to the many initiatives that wouldn't have materialized without her support and/or influence, such as pursuing programs in Africa and Asia.

Dr. Hand knew it would be difficult to give up the influence she had over international education at the university. She had been through the major transitions and played an important role during a difficult time. Why was she thinking of giving it up when things were finally falling into place? On the other hand, her research was starting to get attention at the international level. Dr. Hand's first book on public policy development in Western Europe was still of interest, and her new book project on antidiscrimination policy in the European Union (EU) was extremely timely.

There was a part of her that really wanted to have the time to be a player in the policy arena. With a new government in place in Washington and people Dr. Hand knew taking positions in it, she realized this was the stage of her career when she could actually have an impact on policy, both in the United States and in Europe.

Dr. Hand thought of herself as a rare commodity, an African American woman with good administrative experience who actually liked being a provost. But she also had a passion for her field of work. Her fate was sealed when her president agreed that she could have a one-year leave in order to catch up on her research. Dr. Hand had planned to apply to take leave the year that she took the provost's position and had always regretted not having that opportunity. Dr. Hand knew that she would take the year off, get involved with international policy, pursue her research agenda, and maybe, just maybe, come back to the provost's position in the future.

Questions

1. If you are a young minority woman with a strong research agenda, would you do what Dr. Hand did?
2. Is the provost's position incompatible with doing research?
3. Did Dr. Hand bring change to her institution because of her minority status?
4. Does being a minority help by leading through a diverse lens?
5. What efforts can be pursued to increase minorities in upper administration jobs?

CASE 2: A PROVOST UNDERSTANDING HOW TO
AFFECT A CULTURE OF DIVERSITY ON HIS CAMPUS

Dr. Adikja is a black gay man. He was hired as provost at a very conservative university in the middle of the country. One of his jobs, according to the president and the chair of the university BoT, was to create a culture of diversity on his campus.

In Dr. Adikja's view, diversity is about empowering people. It is not about affirmative action. Those are laws and policies. For him, diversity is understanding, valuing, and using the differences in every person. He always thought that simply enforcing government regulations would not get you to the best culture of diversity. To obtain that, Dr. Adikja needed to grow his work force from groups into teams to use the full potential of every individual.

For Dr. Adikja, teams are much more than a group. A group is collection of individuals where each person is working toward his or her own goal, while a team is a collection of individuals working toward a common goal or vision. This helps to create a synergistic effect with teams, that is, one plus one equals more than one.

An individual, acting alone, can accomplish a lot; but a group of people acting together as a unified force can accomplish great wonders. This is because team members understand each other and support each other in an inclusive manner. Personal agendas do not get in the way of the team's goal.

Embracing diversity is the first item for building teams. Every team building theory states that to build a great team, there must be a diverse group of people on the team, that is, one must avoid choosing people who are only like themselves. Diversity is what builds teams, multiple collections of individual experiences, backgrounds, and cultures that can view problems and challenges from a wide variety of lenses.

For Dr. Adikja, bias and prejudice are deeply rooted within us. From the moment we are born, we begin to learn our environment, the world, and ourselves. Families, friends, peers, books, teachers, idols, and others influence us on what is right and what is wrong. This early learning is deeply rooted within us and shapes our perceptions about how we view things and how we respond to them. What we learn and experience gives us a *subjective point of view* known as *bias*.

Dr. Adikja also thought that our biases serve as filtering lenses that allow us to make sense of new information and experiences based on what we already know. Many of our biases are good as they allow us to assume that something is true without proof. Otherwise, we would have to start learning anew on everything that we do. But, if we allow a bias to shade our perceptions of what people are capable of, then the bias is harmful. We start prejudging others on what we think that they cannot do.

For Dr. Adikja, embracing diversity was more than tolerating people who are different. It meant actively welcoming and involving them by developing an atmosphere that is safe for all, and actively seeking information from people from a variety of backgrounds and cultures. Diversity is not only black and white, female and male, gay and straight, Jewish and Christian, young and old, for example, but the diversity of every individual, slow learner and fast learner, introvert and extrovert, controlling type and people type, scholar and sports-person, liberal and conservative.

This is where Dr. Adikja wanted to focus his energy, helping people to realize that it takes a wide variety of people to become the best and that they need to have the ability to be able to rely on everyone on their team, no matter how different another person may be.

He considered the development of diversity a soft skill. Unlike hard skills, soft skills are relatively hard to evaluate. For him, development was training people to acquire new horizons or viewpoints. It enables him as a leader to guide his university into new expectations by being proactive rather than reactive.

Soft skills generally fall under the domain of attitudes. Soft skill training is mainly changing attitudes, a disposition or tendency to respond positively or negatively toward a certain idea, object, person, or situation. Since our attitudes are deeply rooted, they are very hard to change. This does not mean you cannot go after changing attitudes. It most cases it is a must.

So Dr. Adikja worked hard in his first two years as provost to develop this community of diversity, by creating positive teams and learning how the attitudes of his colleagues was affecting the campus culture. He learned a lot about implicit biases, but he is proud to say that since his arrival his campus has learned to negotiate the multicultural dimensions of diversity and become a better place for students, faculty, staff, and administrators.

Questions

1. Do you agree with Dr. Adikja's definition of diversity?
2. Would you think that teams are the way to build consensus?
3. Do you share Dr. Adikja views on bias and prejudice?
4. What have you done to build the campus diversity different than Dr. Adikja?
5. Do you agree that the concept of diversity is a soft skill?
6. What resources does a minority provost have to increase diversity on his/her campus?

Scenario 1

When Dr. Imani was appointed provost at Gainesville College, she was the first female in the upper administration. She was worried that this would present a challenge, but she was very lucky to work for an African American male president who wanted to diversify his cabinet. He recommended that Dr. Imani join a provost's organization to be with a group of provosts where it was safe to talk about institutional issues and solved problems.

There she met other female provosts who were also the only women in leadership positions on their campuses. In that venue, Dr. Imani discussed the challenges of the provost's position, especially when the rest of the vice presidents were white men and entrenched in their views of senior administration. Fortunately, in her second year as provost, the president hired another woman as vice president of EM and a Latino man as vice president of finance, significantly changing the composition of the cabinet in his goal for cabinet diversity.

Over time, these changes in the senior administration led many on campus to perceive the cabinet as increasingly collegial and appreciative of minority groups.

CASE 3: A LATINO MAN TALKS ABOUT FACTORS THAT AFFECTED HIS CAREER

Dr. Perez was a dean for many years before becoming a provost in a public comprehensive institution. In his years as dean, he attended many meetings of the Council of College of Arts and Sciences (CCAS), where he learned that the movement of Latinos into academic administration positions has been supported by academic supervisors' mentoring and targeted recruitment of minority faculty/staff into those leadership positions. Often, their recruitment into the upper administration was related to having been noticed for their management performance in key university committees.

In Dr. Perez's experience, factors that negatively affected Latino provost career development included workplace climate issues, limited multicultural perspective, and racial or ethnic differences. High academic service demands, insufficient social support, and ongoing discrimination contributed to the slow progress Dr. Perez worked through to move into a provost position. He was determined to address those challenges at his new institution.

Latino provosts, Dr. Perez knew, come in many flavors: language, skin and feature complexion, inherent political views, and socioeconomic status. These bring prejudices due to false perceptions. For example, those of European complexion, until they open their mouths cannot be placed in a Latino culture and there are assumed perceptions because of country of origin regarding one's Latino cultural heritage.

Once it is known that they come from a Latin American country like Argentina, they are frequently pigeonholed into being from a socialist political view with the consequences that may bring. If the perception is Argentina, it is also assumed that they are educated and from a higher socioeconomic status. That is different than if the Latino provost comes from Honduras, Guatemala, or El Salvador, to cite some examples.

Latino provosts (and others) may also be subject to micro-aggressions due to their accents. Sometimes Latino provosts with strong accents are not understood and that leads to frustration in the flow of communication. They may be perceived as less educated or less intelligent than their academic peers.

Dr. Perez knew he needed to work harder to gain the same respect that is normally given to a white person. He had heard comments that he got the job because he was a minority and an affirmative action case, but not because he was the most deserving. He also heard that because of his origin, he might not be able to perform his job as well as his peers because of Latino family pressures and responsibilities.

In his first year as provost, Dr. Perez got an evaluation from his president that he needed to improve his speaking and writing skills because it was hard for the president to understand Dr. Perez's heavy accent and he was aggravated by the thought that this may have been a "poor" hire.

Dr. Perez was also a very collaborative provost and he wanted to include the affected community in decision-making. The president saw this as a weakness, because the president perceived collaboration was lack of leadership.

It took several years for Dr. Perez to change the culture of his institution and be accepted as a good provost. He was able to convince his president that the reason he tended to infuse collaboration and collective leadership was that it enabled him to inspire individual deans and faculty to shared responsibility, joint action, and being mutually accountable. It was a strength and not a weakness. He was able to demonstrate that when he was working with his deans and his departments, fostering this collective leadership, he got better results.

Over time, with this approach Dr. Perez was able to get the institution to view the value of diversification in their upper administration. That brought not only diversity to the institution, but an incredible level of community participation from the Hispanic communities around his institution.

Questions

1. Do you agree with Dr. Perez's statements about the difficulties of being Latino and holding an upper administration job?
2. If you are a minority provost, have you been subject to micro-aggressions?
3. What have you have done different than Dr. Perez?
4. If you are a minority provost, how do you handle your relationships with your counterparts?

CASE 4: STRATEGIES FROM A LATINA
PROVOST TO ENHANCE CAMPUS CLIMATE

Dr. Gonzales was hired as a provost at a small private university. An important role she wanted to play was being a mentor for other Latinas in the institution, leading them to be the new group of administrators in higher education. Dr. Gonzales recognized that her deans and chairpersons were those leading the departments, but that as provost she could play a role in providing guidance in promotion and tenure (especially in increasing faculty diversity), curriculum innovation, research initiatives, and program reviews.

Providing opportunities for Latinas on campus, she thought, could help improve the campus climate for Latinas in a university aspiring for greater inclusiveness.

Dr. Gonzales knew that having a strong deans' team was one of the most successful strategies for accomplishing many of her provost's tasks. A strong deans' team contributes to academic unity across the campus, allows for better understanding among peers, and creates a familiar ground where everyone feels more respected in expressing their own cultural views.

As a Latina provost, she found that a leadership strategy that worked well with her peers when making a team decision was shared-leadership. In using shared-leadership, she focused on behavior that was inclusive and looked to enrich all, promoting behaviors where all members of a team were fully engaged. When guiding departments as a member of a minority group, Dr. Gonzales always infused collaboration and collective leadership, and inspired individual faculty to shared responsibility, joint action, and mutual accountability.

For instance, in a particular search undertaken by an all-white department, Dr. Gonzales was able to help the dean use a collaborative approach with the department to see the value of diversification. They hired an African American faculty member that brought not only diversity to the department, but also a strong sense of community participation from the African American communities around her institution.

As a Latina provost, she always provided her deans with chances to share and participate. She encouraged an open, respectful, and informed conversation, which was central to the success of any action item the team decided on. Through listening and contributing, thoughts and ideas emerged and developed, and Dr. Gonzales liked to emphasize that it was not her position as provost that was necessarily important but the behavior of the team that promoted actions to achieve success. This allowed the team to understand and experience cultural differences while solving issues.

Although challenges existed, Dr. Gonzales found ample benefits from her shared-leadership style. This allowed her to identify the quality of her deans' team's interactions rather than the individual positions of each of the deans. For Dr. Gonzales, teamwork promoted a more fulfilling process, one that led to interdependent team works with better communications, values honesty, and shared ethics in seeking common goals.

Since the university where Dr. Gonzales was hired as provost was not diverse, she was seen as different during the earlier part of her tenure because she was an outsider that needed to be "checked out." Because of her Latina mannerisms, her loud voice, and her way of expressing herself, she was perceived as having a "big personality." Over time, her deans and fellow VPs welcomed her cultural "differences" because she helped them expand their horizons. By sharing her heritage stories, she enhanced the groups and enriched the workplace, and she was accepted because of her warm personality as a Latina.

Dr. Gonzales was perceived as partial to promoting certain academic programs over others. She was the only Latina in upper administration participating in many university-wide diversity events. She was very supportive of initiating a Global Studies Program in the School of Liberal Arts and Sciences.

The perception of her president was that she wanted to move the school in a global direction because she was Latina and biased toward globalization. Luckily, she was able to convince her president of the importance of increasing the global aspects of the university. She also had very difficult conversations with her president, such as pointing out that lower salary compensation was being given to minority hires.

As a Latina provost, Dr. Gonzales had limited access to mentoring and social support networks, which could have hindered her career advancement. So she took it upon herself to strengthen efforts to combat the social isolation of a Latina provost by becoming very active in a provost organization and increasing cross-institutional collaborations within the larger academy. She learned through shared stories that the potential for Latinas to be recruited into upper administrative jobs and be retained in those jobs depended on prior administrative experience, motivation, networking, and mentoring opportunities.

Dr. Gonzales made a concerted effort to bring those qualities to the few Latina faculty in her institution to help increase the representation of Latinas in higher education administration. She also worked at educating her non-Latino counterparts about the rapidly growing Latino population in the United States.

Questions

1. Do you agree with Dr. Gonzales's leadership style for success?
2. Was Dr. Gonzales biased when she promoted the Global Studies Program?

3. If you are a minority provost, do you encounter similar issues, such as lower salaries for minority faulty, that Dr. Gonzales did? If so, what can you do about it?
4. Do you agree with Dr. Gonzales joining and actively participating in the provost organization?
5. Is there enough mentoring for minority provosts?

Scenario 2

Provost Zambula works at a university in the middle of the country that has for years been trying to attract more minority faculty members. This issue has taken on new urgency in the last two years as minority student protests have demanded a more diversified faculty. Provost Zambula, being a minority himself, has made a pledge to hire more minority professors.

One serious concern Provost Zambula has about making progress on his pledge is the fact that in his institution faculty hiring decisions are approved by the individual department chairs. So, Provost Zambula had mixed feelings about the realism of his own targets, even though he wants to complete the institution goal.

Provost Zambula read in a study in the Chronicle of Higher Education that members of underrepresented minority groups held approximately 16 percent of faculty jobs in 2016, up from 9 percent in 1993, and only holds 10 percent of tenured jobs. The students at his institution had demanded hires in faculty ranks, not adjunct positions.

Provost Zambula's institution has specific targets for increasing the number of minority faculty members, and he felt the departments were trying hard. In a meeting with the deans, Provost Zambula found out that only 53 percent of the chairs agreed with the minority initiative. Provost Zambula knew that his institution would need to make hiring decisions in new ways in order to achieve the goal of increases in the number of minority faculty members.

Provost Zambula believed that a way to move forward was working with faculty members on the curriculum, another area where students were concerned about diversity. He had wide support for efforts to add courses and programs related to diversity and for requiring undergraduates to take courses that in some way focus on diversity. He felt that updating the curriculum with this perspective would lead to securing more minority positions in the future.

FINAL THOUGHTS

What you do has far greater impact than what you say.

—Stephen Covey

One of the successes of diversity is the inclusion of all. If inclusion is not present, diversity may be achievable, but not sustainable. A lack of belonging for each and every member adversely impacts an institution. Both diversity and inclusion start at the top. People need role models who look like them at the top of institution, so they feel they are represented and know there is room for them to grow and succeed at the academy.

They need to be inspired by leaders who understand diversity and inclusion. But having a diverse leadership team isn't just about role models. It also addresses similarity-attraction bias: people's tendency to be attracted to, and hire, others who are similar to themselves. We believe that the academy could benefit by including men in the conversation about women, white employees in the conversation about black, Latino, and Asian employees, heterosexual employees in the conversation about gay, lesbian, and transgender employees, and including all employees in the conversation about disabled, deaf, and blind employees.

The academy should make a concentrated effort to hire people of different races, genders, ages, and sexual orientations not only because it "looks good" but also because it encourages a wide range of perspectives. With today's ever-changing workplace landscape, that diversity of perspective is crucial for succeeding and staying ahead. And you as a provost have a critical role in facilitating the hiring of diverse faculty and staff in the academic affairs division.

Although no one individual is responsible for creating an inclusive culture, your leadership team ultimately sets the tone for the entire division. You are in a leadership position, so if you want to see change in your institution, you need first to reflect on your own behavior and biases.

Are you publicly praising all deserving employees for their outstanding work and providing recognition as often as it's earned? Diversity is not an issue that just affects minorities or women. Diversity is an issue that affects the entire workforce. Diversity should factor the level of equality and access to the same mentors, advisers, faculty, and advocates. Engaging people with differing perspectives in a synergistic process that produces exponential results is the goal of any academic collaboration.

However, whenever there is a diversity of opinions and perspectives, arguments and disagreements are inevitable; they are a necessary part of the collaboration process, as this process will bring critical change at the end. Seeking out diverse candidates isn't hard. Recruiting those candidates and placing them in an environment where different backgrounds, cultures, and experiences are appreciated is more difficult. Retaining diverse faculty is perhaps the largest challenge.

If your institution creates an environment where diverse faculty can be successful, those same faculty become "targets" for recruitment by other institutions that are trying to diversify. If a university has done this correctly, it should be reflected in the makeup of the management team. Once a university has this kind of environment, diverse candidates will come and stay.

Always remember that even with the best of intentions, you may say or do something that sounds more exclusionary than inclusionary. We are all humans and we all have our own biases. If you can, call yourself out first. Otherwise, deal with any backlash sooner rather than later. Keep in mind that the road to hell is often paved with good intentions. We humans are a work in progress, especially when we're trying to create a more inclusive workplace.

Chapter 4

Balancing Academic and Institutional Priorities

This chapter addresses the fact that the provost typically is the chief academic officer and often must advocate for academic program and resource issues as well as support students, faculty, and deans. At the same time, larger institutional concerns and realities must be communicated to the academic division. Negotiating with other senior administrators requires astute psychology and understanding of human motivation, emotions, and responses to ideas and issues.

For public universities, academic and institutional priorities in some cases will exist in relationship with the priorities of a board managing a multicampus university system, or a statewide board of regents. In those cases, the system or statewide board will articulate what it believes are overarching goals on such topics as affordability, access, and course credit portability.

The challenge for a new provost is to understand the relationship between those system or state goals and the practice and priorities of the provost's own institution. In some states, even private universities may find themselves needing to deal frequently with a state agency. Be sure to explore such regulatory oversight if you move from one state to another when you assume the role of provost.

A related concern for public university provosts can be direct work with state government or state agencies, which may articulate priorities and policies directly relevant to everyday management of the academic units. State human resources offices, for example, may implement rules for the state with the potential to greatly complicate temporary staff hiring, or the adjustment of salaries for highly skilled staff employees.

Provosts may also be asked to interact directly with legislators, usually along with the president or the chair of the BoT. In such interactions, provosts

43

might be called to comment directly on matters of university policy, instructional practice, or institutional mission. Such questions may have relevance to institutional priorities, especially when a legislator's question is directly pertinent to the budget of the university. Provosts in such cases should be carefully prepared for legislative interactions, complete with advance briefings, if possible from a university lobbyist or public affairs liaison.

At private universities, the dynamics may involve members of boards of trustees who are either alumni or members of the local business community. In these cases, there may be deep and conflicting loyalties related to the past identity of the university, particularly if the institution has undergone radical changes such as the admission of previously excluded groups of students (gender, religion, etc.) or changes in mission (such as a liberal arts institution offering professional programs or graduate programs).

A provost needs to understand the personal history of board members and their involvement with the university, including their history of donations. Such information can often be obtained from the development office or an alumni affairs officer. In the case of community business leaders, it is important to understand professional background and motivation for being part of the board. In some cases, community members will have a genuine interest in how the university supports the community; in other cases, board membership may be a matter of vanity, social position, or resume enhancement.

It is also vital for a provost to understand the president's interactions with the board and to be certain that board members do not try to circumvent the president. Be sure to keep your president in the loop about interactions with your board, regardless of whether yours is a public or a private university.

WORKING WITH THE CABINET

If one has come up through the faculty ranks, as professor, chair, and dean, it is easy to see that the academic mission of the institution is the raison d'être for the institution. It may seem straightforward that the other senior officers of the institution are there to serve the academic mission.

Unfortunately, all other members of the president's cabinet seldom share this viewpoint. Whether in a public or a private institution, limited resources will result in each vice president focusing, at least some of the time, on the needs of their own units without considering the academic context. In order to be successful, a provost will need to negotiate with these vice presidents to find common ground.

Examples

1. *Chief Financial Officer (CFO)*—a CFO will be driven by bottom-line considerations and will see that some aspects of academic quality—smaller class sizes, stronger faculty (who command higher salaries), more academic advisers, centers for faculty development—are expensive and result in no direct return on investment. Some will also be focused on managing year to year rather than focusing on long-term investment.

   Here, the provost's ability to speak financial language, read a balance sheet, and provide quantitative projections of revenue and expense will be essential in establishing a good rapport with the CFO. Demonstrating your ability to find savings when necessary can also sometimes help convince the CFO that you are a good steward of institutional resources. Some academic associations (ACE, CIC[1]) offer conferences that CFOs and provosts can attend together, as a sort of "retreat," which may be valuable in developing trust.

2. *Vice President (VP) for Enrollment or Admissions*—it is important to understand what goals the institution has set for this VP in order to find common ground. In a public institution whose budget comes from the state, the VP may be focused more on diversity, retention and/or graduation rates—which can be fertile ground for collaboration. In a tuition-driven private institution (or in many publics these days), net revenue from tuition may be the primary driver, at the expense of academic quality.

   Here again, data may be helpful, and things you can do to show that academic affairs is willing to roll up its sleeves to improve net tuition revenue through quality-enhancing measures will improve your relationship with EM. This unit often has direct contact with faculty, particularly if EM includes the registrar's office or if faculty are often called upon to engage in recruiting efforts, and it is important for the provost to both support and appreciate these efforts, and possibly mediate if trouble arises.

3. *Student Affairs*—this unit can be both the most rewarding and the most challenging to collaborate with. Unlike the other units, this one has substantial direct contact with students (particularly on a residential campus). This can be fertile ground for collaboration, since both academic and student affairs tend to have student success as a goal.

   At the same time, many faculty will be underappreciative, or even hostile, toward student affairs efforts which are seen as not-rigorous, or because student affairs deals with student discipline, Title IX, and other

---

[1] American Council on Education, Council of Independent Colleges.

difficult areas. Faculty may also be hostile to student affairs units such as disability services if they believe that these units either provide not enough service or are artificially enabling weak students.

A history of such conflicts can lead student affairs leaders to be suspicious of academic affairs. In some institutions, student affairs will have direct oversight of quasi-academic units such as academic advising or tutoring, which also requires that the provost build a strong relationship "across the aisle."

Scenario 1

Dr. Bustion became provost at her institution where she had worked for many years. She understood her new role as an advocate for academic affairs, and she needed to relate the importance of academic priorities to the other VP's and the president. Dr. Bustion's first step was to form alliances with the budget director to ensure that he fully understood the academic needs of the institution. Her division also developed an academic master plan so that she would have evidenced-based information to make her case for additional resources.

It was fortunate that the president and the cabinet agreed that academic resources needed to be protected to an appropriate extent. That didn't mean that there were no academic cuts, just that those decisions were well thought out and consistent with strategic priorities, and the subsequent ramifications were fully understood. To be sure everyone accepted the academic priorities, Dr. Bustion met individually on a regular basis with each cabinet member.

Fully understanding the needs of her colleagues helped her to be supportive of their initiatives and in return, they supported academic affairs. Her interactions with the other VPs also helped to make collegial decisions at the cabinet level, always considering what was best for the institution as the ultimate goal.

CHANGING CEREMONIAL OCCASIONS

The annual ceremonies at a college or university such as commencement and honors convocations are some of the most difficult events to change but they can be very costly. While they may look attractive as a way to achieve quick budget savings, they tend to be laden with tradition and ritual, highly complex, and often emotionally charged for faculty and often for administrators.

Students will also have a decided opinion, but since students "turn over" each year, it is often possible to innovate if other supporters can be brought on board. On the other hand, new alumni may leave the institution with a bad taste in their mouths if the culmination of their degrees is not the ceremony they imagined. While academic affairs may have formal charge of the planning, every other VP will need to weigh in on changes that may be contemplated.

CASE 1: A PROVOST DEALING WITH COMMENCEMENT CEREMONIES

Provost Chen has come to a private institution in the rainy Pacific Northwest from a stint as a dean, and previously a faculty member at public universities in the Midwest. He discovers soon after arriving that the university's budget is in bad shape, and his president orders him to implement cost-cutting measures immediately. One item in Provost Chen's budget looks ripe for trimming—the high cost of the spring commencement ceremony.

At his previous schools, graduation had been an outdoor, rain or shine "mass commencement" in which individual students are not recognized but degrees are conferred in large groups. Provost Chen's new institution is under pressure to provide the personal experience of giving each student their opportunity to walk across a stage and shake the hand of the president.

To make sure that commencement happens "rain or shine" and that parents who have just paid a small fortune for their child's education are not sitting in the broiling sun or a downpour while waiting to see their child graduate, a tradition had developed of pitching a large, commercial tent on the quad and holding two commencement ceremonies on separate days inside the tent.

In addition, the school has a long-standing tradition of holding the honors convocation in the university's tiny chapel on the day before both spring commencement ceremonies. The honors convocation has become unwieldy. As the quality of students at the institution has increased, the number of students qualifying to participate has increased to the point where they and their audience cannot fit.

A proposal supported by the VP for facilities as well as student affairs to hold the honors convocation in the roomier tent involves less time and money on logistics, but adds to the expense by leaving the tent in place for additional days. The VP for alumni affairs objects because the tent is not as attractive an option, and many of her best donors come from the ranks of honors students and their families.

Options included doing commencement on the quad without the tent, renting a nearby arena for a single ceremony for all, or combining the two ceremonies and changing the procession to make it more time-efficient.

Students have gotten wind of the options being explored and have actively protested all the proposed changes, despite efforts to include student representatives in discussions of alternatives. Faculty, especially from disciplines with significant graduate programs, objected to combining ceremonies, fearing that the graduate students would not feel as special at the (inevitably longer) combined ceremony. The president objects to combining the honors convocation with commencement—she feels that an overflowing honors event sends a great message about institutional quality.

Questions

1. What kind of timeline for decision-making processes should Provost Chen implement?
2. Who should be "at the table" in the decision-making process?
3. What do you think his communication plan should look like—both during and after the decision-making process, and at the time of the ceremony if there is a "rain plan" that needs to be in place?
4. What institutional values come into play in a decision such as this one? Can tradition outweigh economy?

Scenario 2

At ARC University, the president did not have the support of his BoT. The president went against the BoT in bringing the university to a higher level of faculty achievement, and there was growing animosity between the president and the faculty who called for a vote of no confidence. The board asked the provost to take a leading role with the faculty and intervene with the faculty senate to avoid a vote of no confidence that could tarnish the reputation of the university.

The provost felt uncomfortable with the BoT's request, but he also knew that to save the university from bankruptcy he needed to engage his faculty in doing more research and better teaching in order to compete with other private universities growing in the surrounding area. His approach to the situation was to create a council of tenured faculty and delegate them to craft a new policy handbook for faculty, with new expectations for excellence in research and teaching.

By delegating this task to senior faculty, the provost earned the respect of the faculty, and after a long year of work, deliberations, and open forums, the faculty senate approved the new handbook almost unanimously.

The BoT commended the provost, but his relationship with his president was damaged. The following year, the BoT fired the current president and hired a new president. With fresh eyes, the president reviewed the work of the provost and named him the executive VP for academic affairs, recognizing his good work with the faculty and the success of the university.

CASE 2: NEW PROVOST IS PROMOTED
AND THE CHANGE IS CHALLENGING

Dr. Gloria was appointed provost at a small private international American-style university in Europe, where he rose through the administrative ranks. Dr. Gloria is an EU citizen who has taught in multiple European countries. On the provost's retirement, Dr. Gloria was chosen to succeed him. He was keen to do the job well and immediately signed up for a summer ACE[2] Institute for new provosts so he could prepare himself as fully as possible.

Dr. Gloria was in his new job for three months when it became apparent that all was not going well. Enrollments were significantly down. This was very bad news for a small institution that depended on tuition dollars for 99 percent of its income. The president, who had announced he would be leaving at the end of the next academic year, had confidently forecast healthy enrollments and built strong spending into his budget, but it soon became apparent that the university would have to confront a potentially disastrous revenue situation, compounded by an unfavorable exchange rate.

The president was asked by the board to step down, and Dr. Gloria, who had considerable support from faculty and staff, was asked to step up as interim president to try to get the university back on track and to allow it to complete its search for a new president. None of the faculty and very few of the administrative staff knew how bad the situation was.

It was clear to Dr. Gloria that he did not have previous experience in running an institution, so the board wisely created a "kitchen cabinet" with which Dr. Gloria worked closely and held conference calls each week. Dr. Gloria was given a short time to draw up a recovery plan with his team and with the advice of the kitchen cabinet, and this would then be considered by the full board.

The plan included downsizing of administrative and academic staff, voluntary pay reductions, tough renegotiation of rents and other contracts. On the positive side, Dr. Gloria built in an advertising campaign to attract local students and extensive travel by the senior team to recruit from their study abroad partners in the United States.

Dr. Gloria began implementing all the obvious budget savings that had been identified and commissioned an independent firm of accountants to determine the university's exact fiscal position. They also calculated the financial effects of the proposed measures in the recovery plan, verifying the CFO's calculations and whether the plan would achieve what it set out to do. The board also wanted to know the best time to close the university in the event that it was no longer viable.

---

[2] American Council on Education.

Dr. Gloria worked with the accountants to model scenarios in which the university was able to pay as many creditors as possible and reduce outstanding liabilities to a minimum. At the same time, he began work on a communication plan for what they would tell students and when, and a teach-out plan which would allow students to either complete their degrees or transfer to other institutions. Dr. Gloria was able to present evidence from the independent review along with the recovery plan, which was subsequently approved.

The process helped consolidate the board's trust in him and his team and gave them the confidence that the solutions they were proposing could work. Dr. Gloria also sought legal advice to ascertain what the board's responsibilities would be if the institution failed and how its officers would be held accountable.

Once the board had approved it, Dr. Gloria's task was to implement the plan rigorously and according to a schedule that would maximize savings. Within a few months it became clear that the university was achieving the results it needed. It also became clear that enrollment both of the study abroad students and of degree students was picking up, either as a consequence of their recruitment efforts, an improved dollar-euro exchange rate, or just the cyclical ups and downs of study abroad numbers.

This meant that Dr. Gloria was able to return the university to normal operational activity, with a deficit within acceptable limits at the end of the first fiscal year. Through continued tight fiscal management, Dr. Gloria achieved a small surplus at the end of the second year. From this he was able to pay back in full the proportion of their salaries to those members of the university who had voluntarily sacrificed when asked.

The transition from new provost to interim president was a true baptism by fire for Dr. Gloria. He found himself in an extreme situation in which many, including officers of the board across the Atlantic in the United States, thought the university was on the point of failure and imminent closure. In a space of eighteen months, he learned much about himself, about the colleagues he had worked with at this small institution, and about the university itself.

Dr. Gloria had learned just how fragile the business model and finances of the university were, and realized the buoyant study abroad market had masked the underlying weaknesses apparent since the 2008 financial crisis. He realized that bold plans had far outstripped university resources and that a number of long-term issues concerning its in-country legal status had not been addressed. Dr. Gloria was not confident that all issues could be resolved satisfactorily in the foreseeable future.

During this period, the search for a new president was successfully completed. Even as the university was celebrating success, Dr. Gloria realized that his relationship with the place he had fought so hard to save and with the people who worked there had been irrevocably altered. His own belief in the university's future had been undermined by what he had seen and learned about it over eighteen months, and he could no longer see a long-term future for himself there.

Although he still had an important job to do as provost in helping the college achieve its first full regional accreditation, he could no longer commit to the place in the same way and he realized that sooner, rather than later, he would have to move on.

After the crisis, Dr. Gloria was struck by how quickly "normality" reasserted itself and was soon just taken for granted, so that the memory of what the institution had just been through seemed to fade completely within a few months. The excitement at having a new president prevailed, and the president in turn was critical of the failures of the board and institutional leaders to grow the university.

Many older members of the board opted to stand down in this transition period and, as new members joined, ambitious plans for growth and development began to surface again, but not backed by sufficient resources nor addressing the fundamental weaknesses in the university's business model, and not sufficiently informed by the need to avoid previous errors in building ambitious annual budgets on volatile study abroad enrollment projections.

Questions

1. Would you have taken the position of interim president if you were Dr. Gloria at the time that the university was quickly spiraling out of control?
2. Would you take a risky plan to the BoT, like the plan Dr. Gloria proposed?
3. Do you think that serving institutions outside of the United States presents different challenges? Why?
4. What did Dr. Gloria learn as interim president? Would you have learned the same lessons? Why or why not?
5. Do you agree with Dr. Gloria's decision to move on? Why or why not?

Scenario 3

Coming from nursing education into the provost's role provided Dr. Daria with experience addressing small faculty/student ratios in clinical courses and how to balance that through massing of other sections. She had managed considerations such as accreditation, especially student outcomes, all levels of assessment, data analysis, and continuous quality improvement, faculty development and support, student synthesis of knowledge and skills development and assessment, and dealing with state agencies such as public safety and professional regulatory boards which have additional programmatic oversight.

Specialty accreditation and state-level regulation prepare nursing faculty who become provosts well for other specialty and regional accreditation. The first accreditation Dr. Daria faced in the provost role was engineering. Her prior experience helped her to quickly understand the engineering accreditation standards, ask key questions of the dean, assess how the school of engineering was meeting the standards, and generally prepare for the site visit.

Provost Daria felt confident that the school was ready and that she could support the visit. Her president, whose background was in the humanities, was initially very concerned that Provost Daria had not delved deeply enough into the accreditation self-study documents and castigated her in front of the entire cabinet.

Later that day, Provost Daria took the multiple bound documents into her office and summarized her assessment. Several days later, she returned to explain to the president that likely because of her experience with professional education accreditation, she was able to easily evaluate the school's readiness.

The second accreditation issue Provost Daria faced had to do with regional accreditation and the need for additional reports and the threat of probation. The issue was prior lack of success in showing that the institution met the standard for strategic planning and implementation. The situation resulted in a nine-month window for creating a new strategic plan and implementation strategy, which Provost Daria led with a faculty and staff steering committee. She knew from prior strategic planning experience that a consultant was needed.

Provost Daria walked a fine line with her president on this effort, being careful not to dismiss prior work or diminish her leadership. Ultimately, the college ended up with a path to strategic effectiveness and a regional accreditation commendation.

Scenario 4

Provost Hakim's home department, the Department of Economics, Finance, and Management, at his new institution, is one that has recently become popular, due to employment prospects for students who successfully complete its programs. Because faculty hiring has not kept pace with demand, during summer orientation new students who need to enroll in the introductory economics sequence often have difficulty finding seats, although in recent years they have been accommodated by the time the semester begins in mid-August.

The director of admissions often complains to the president that the department is not responsive enough to the needs of new students, and he is concerned that more and more students will "melt" prior to the beginning of the semester if they cannot make schedules during their assigned orientation dates. The department has been reluctant to change its practices since, in the eyes of the chair and faculty, the issues are generally resolved by the time classes begin. The president orders Provost Hakim to find ways to make the registration of students in the program easier.

The provost feels that he needs to work through the new dean of the division in which the program lies, even though the dean is new to the institution and comes from the arts, so that her expertise in the issue is much less than that of the provost. Provost Hakim wants to be sure that the new dean is seen by the faculty as in charge and empowered; he also wants to be sure that the president and the admissions office go through chain of command and are not unduly pressuring the dean to make poor decisions.

Scenario 5

Provost Isaacson of Riley State University has joined President Longespee for the president's testimony before the Higher Education Committee of the State House of Representatives. The committee will be voting soon on budget recommendations for higher education institutions, including Riley State. A representative asks repeatedly why Riley State is the only public university in the state that requires two years of foreign-language education for general education (GE) and, as a result, will not accept a community college AA or AS degree in lieu of fulfilling Riley's GE requirements.

President Longespee, a former business leader, states that foreign-language instruction is an institutional priority for Riley, but she struggles to explain why foreign-language instruction is important for all students in applied and professional disciplines like accounting. The legislator asks President Longespee if the president would endorse an amendment to the state budget requiring Riley to accept AA and AS degrees as fully satisfying GE requirements, even though such degrees generally do not include foreign-language instruction.

The president responds that the faculty had recently voted against such a transfer policy for holders of associate's degrees. The legislator expresses disappointment with the president's response and asks Provost Isaacson to comment on the faculty's position, which the legislator maintains is "obviously hostile to students and to their families."

FINAL THOUGHTS

The most difficult thing is the decision to act, the rest is merely tenacity.

—Amelia Earhart

A key challenge faced by a provost is to convince other institutional leaders of the critical role that academic affairs plays in better fulfilling the overall mission of the institution. Many times, provosts express their frustration about the lack of understanding of their peer VPs, the president, or the BoT regarding the extremely difficult challenges associated with the management of academic affairs, in particular about unlimited priorities and ideas while restricted by resource limitations.

All too often, the academic agenda is perceived by other administrators as one of those ideas which can be labeled as a priority to be addressed in the future when better times arise and more resources become available. Ideally, a common shared goal (or dream?) is to find the key formula that will help each division in the institution to become a more meaningful player. But in most cases, each division administrator expressed their frustrations to gain the attention, interest and, of course, allocation of resources in institutional decision-making.

Is there any common ground between academic priorities and institutional priorities? Are there ways to bring together both perspectives? Is there room for dialogue between provosts and their peer VPs and president? Those are critical questions you should ask yourself as a provost.

Your job is to find common ground in recognizing the importance of the academic division in higher education. For some VPs, the role of academic affairs may simply mean the availability of graduates with adequate skills. For your faculty members, their division is the most important part of the institution, from both educational and research perspectives. For your students, this is their academic home and a way to succeed in their future careers. For the president, sometimes it means prestige, position in the rankings, or an opportunity to obtain additional revenue streams for the institution.

Your job as a provost is to manage all those expectations when prioritizing academic initiatives with other institutional initiatives. Fortunately, there are some very encouraging cases of higher education institutions where academic affairs becomes the main pillar of the institutional strategic plan, the fulfillment of institutional goals, and the main division to prepare socially responsible citizens not only locally but globally.

Chapter 5

Assessing the Fit of Your Team

This chapter discusses the role of a well-functioning team in the academic operation division. Assessing the "fit" of the team requires an understanding of its members, creating a shared vision, and a team willingness to implement the necessary action steps to bring that vision to a reality. Provosts need to regularly assess the contributions and strengths of each team member and must be willing to make difficult decisions when there is a need to make personnel changes. We include stories of implementing shared governance and administering resource allocation within academic affairs.

A provost is responsible for a very large number of employees. Most provosts, unless they have a very narrow scope, are going to have 60 to 70 percent of the university under their umbrella. Consequently, team fit has multiple dimensions and, in this conversation, it is about an array of adjustments that can be made managerially.

First of all, it is the portfolio of assets that each individual represents and asking, "How do I get the most out of each individual person?" A provost must then figure out how to forge relationships to make the team he or she has to work and then simultaneously ask, "How do I make this work better in the future?" That might mean additional professional development, it might mean particular kinds of mentoring, it might mean giving a person more autonomy, and it might mean giving them less—so there are a host of ways to maximize what you get from each person. In fact, it might mean giving that person a different portfolio.

For example, say you have somebody reporting to you who has five distinct responsibilities. They're great at three of them, middling at the fourth, and awful at the fifth. You might carve that up. In a few cases, you recognize that this conversation about the individual is really an organizational conversation.

It is not that the individual can't do effective work at a high level for you, it's that they're doing some of the wrong things or all of the wrong things and then you have to find a way to ask, "Can I find a way to make a good use of this individual?" But you may have to reorganize to get there.

So fit for a team to make a provost maximally effective is everything from an administrative assistant all the way to the deans and the vice presidents who might report directly to the provost. The team has to be imagined as everyone around the provost who reports to the provost or reports to someone and reports to the provost indirectly. All of these people are essential to productivity and output.

In addition, there may be "team members" who do not report to the provost but whose close alliance with the provost's office make cultivating them (and their bosses) essential to consider when thinking about the structure of the team. These might be individuals whose reporting line is to another VP (such as a registrar or head of disability services) but whose work is closely allied with academics. It might also be elected representatives of faculty—Senate committee chairs, union heads, and so on—whose role under certain circumstances becomes part of a team effort to accomplish a goal.

Communication should be integral to a provost's assessment and ongoing management. Communication that enables you to extract critical information focuses on listening, listening, and listening. With regards to the executive and senior personnel decisions that a provost might make, part of the challenge of the new position is trying to assess how long people have been there, what they say their strengths and weaknesses are, and what others say about their strengths and weaknesses. Be aware that that these different perspectives frequently do not align with each other.

It usually is not difficult to get people to talk about their work. People of seniority on your team are generally self-aware, so they can effectively answer the question, "What are my weaknesses?" The prompts you ask and the initial conversations, whether it's before you take the job or right after you take the job, are very straightforward. The challenge for a new provost is to keep his or her mouth shut for as long as possible because they'll keep talking.

People who are mediocre will eventually reveal themselves. You give people a chance to tell you their story, you ask general questions, and you listen to get what you need. The biggest danger a new provost has in this area is trying to solve a problem too quickly. The question is, can you get the information you need to do this very complicated job well over the long haul? It generally means listening longer than you thought you needed to.

Remember that anyone who is going to be at the senior or executive level has considerable talent or they wouldn't have gotten there. But if they have the wrong strengths for the job and you want retraining or realignment that is not going to be possible or practical, then you've either got to find them something else to do or help them move on. Your goal, if someone must be sent back to the faculty, is to have them thank you for doing it. In many systems, whether public or private, retirement or termination is so difficult and so harmful to team morale, or so potentially fraught with threat of litigation, that you try to find other solutions.

Getting rid of team members is a tiny percentage of the work because most of the time you're trying to help the people you already have do their work better or help them to understand that their work could be better. Don't hesitate to recommend professional development for anyone on your team whom you think will benefit. In some cases, you may discover you have someone who is absolutely wonderful in their work from your perspective and all you need to do is get out of their way: sometimes by empowering them to do more than they're currently empowered to do.

As far as these fit challenges are concerned, they go well beyond those constantly in your orbit. It's also the five faculty who are the top producers with NSF grants, the people who just created something patentable, it's the person who just wrote the novel on your creative writing faculty that hit the *New York Times* best seller list and is unhappy and talking about leaving the same week that happens. So the question is how do you help those people who are frankly trying to go around the dean and the chair?

The solution is normally a lot of communication. The person has asked to meet because he or she is unsatisfied. If you know this person is a significant player in their unit and you may be able to help with a solution, make the appointment. If you make the appointment, make sure the dean and chair know you are having this conversation. This lets them know from the beginning this is not a "behind the back" conversation. Talk to the dean with an admonition to inform the chair. Make very clear that the solution, if there is one to whatever problem may be defined, is going to go through the dean.

The longer a provost is in place, the more deans realize that there are not going to be any surprises and the more capital (trust) is accumulated, the easier it is to do that. The challenge for the new provost, who hasn't got any capital at all at this point, is to build that trust with direct reports who don't want to have the sense that the provost is going to overrule them every day.

To get work done well with your team requires constant maintenance of trust and a set of priorities for how you work. Provosts must be clear on what it is that they are trying to do well, and perhaps most importantly, how they're trying to get better at it. So the fit of the team is as much about understanding where you are going directionally and making sure that is the underlying theme of everything you do as you work with one another.

Fit questions are finally about bringing together the organization and its priorities, which deans do not set and provosts do not set. All have a role to play, but the president and the board will have the final say. A provost can be terrific at what she or he does well, but if the institution is not going there, the provost is going to be miserable in the long run. Discerning that direction is difficult because there's what was heard in the interview, there's what the strategic plan or the mission statement says, and there's the reality that is on campus.

Sometimes a new provost arrives and finds the mission is exactly right and everyone is aligned and going toward the same place. Other times, the new provost finds out the minority voices are powerful. The inertia aligned against the strategic plan is considerable and everything that happens that is good will die the moment the president leaves. This can be death to the morale and the effectiveness of any provost. The answer is back to communication.

A provost needs to talk to as many people as possible, in as unstructured environment as possible, very early in the process. The first five or twenty people who talk to the provost are usually going to be in positions of authority, but they're not going to have the same perspective as the institution. They are going to be better informed in some ways because they are insiders with the current administration but they are not going to represent the full range of diversity or belief about the institution and its future. They may not always be reliable informants on some of the people elsewhere in the organization whom they do not want to cross.

So how does one weigh the feedback from the various entities? That is why experienced academics are hired to be provosts. People who understand that there are agenda that come with every conversation involving the provost and that some informants are more reliable than others. Aim for a wide range of conversations so that you can compare one narrative to another. It is difficult to explain the dynamics of provosts' relationships to other people because provosts exist in a web of relationships with people who have considerable individual autonomy and great security of employment as faculty.

Scenario 1

When Dr. Sukumaran was appointed provost, she needed to evaluate the office team. She had worked with this team as an associate provost, so the relationship building was already in place. Dr. Sukumaran needed to bring in a new associate provost to fill the spot she vacated and chose an individual with faculty and leadership experience with whom she had worked in other capacities. There were some reassignments of responsibilities among existing staff, so that individuals were working to their strengths. Dr. Sukumaran believed it was a very skilled and cohesive team.

Scenario 2

Dr. Enue was appointed provost at a small college in a rural area. The prior provost had been in the job for over twenty years with the same office staff. Dr. Enue had learned how to manage her office team from her many years as dean and she knew what she was looking for on her new team. When she arrived on her new job, she knew immediately that she needed to make changes not only in personnel but also on how the business of the provost's office was conducted. One of the areas that took Dr. Enue lots of time was to train her administrative assistant on how she wanted her calendar.

Dr. Enue also needed to make difficult decisions about her office staff. One of the most crucial decisions was to terminate her associate provost. He had also been there for close to twenty years and was too set in his ways. They clashed often, and her only recourse was to terminate him. That was very difficult for some of the secretarial staff in the office. Dr. Enue knew then that she needed to remove one of the senior secretaries. Dr. Enue denied her promotion and was able to negotiate moving her to another division.

One of Dr. Enue's senior deans complained to the president about the changes she was making in her office staff. It was a difficult transition process, but Dr. Enue knew she needed to have an office team she could depend on and gets the things done in an efficient and quality manner.

CASE 1: UNDERMINING ACCREDITATION

A small, budget-starved, private university has been placed on warning by its accreditor, but it falls to the new provost, Dr. Kali, to continue the process for writing a new self-study and hosting a site visit that must reaffirm accreditation. A new president is on board that is very popular with some faculty but very unpopular with many "old guard" faculty and administrators. An interim provost had assembled a small steering committee of faculty and administrators to guide the self-study process and assemble the final document.

Provost Kali takes over the role of chairing the steering committee and works diligently to keep the process moving forward while the associate provost, Dr. Main, who has served a succession of provosts for the past twenty years, handles the day-to-day organization of the process. As the work goes on, Provost Kali feels that there is a reasonable chance that the institution will achieve reaccreditation despite many difficulties.

A few weeks before the self-study is due to the accreditation agency, Provost Kali receives a call from one of the faculty on the steering committee requesting a meeting. He brings to the meeting a staff member; both of them are supporters of the new president. They report that Associate Provost Main has pressured them to include material that suggests that the new president is not doing her job, material that both believe is false. They ask Provost Kali for support in resisting the request to include the questionable material. The provost assures them that she will support them, given the lack of evidence for the assertions of the associate provost.

At the next meeting of the steering committee, when it is time to approve all the chapters and pass them to the senior faculty member who has volunteered to edit them, Provost Kali is surprised when the editor withdraws, leaving a few weeks before the self-study is due. Associate Provost Main has been the hands-on manager of the process on the provost's behalf, but seems unwilling to come up with suggestions for how to proceed without an editor. Main's behavior reinforces the provost's feeling that the associate provost is working to derail the reaccreditation process, which may result in the downfall of the new president and the new provost.

At this point, the provost alerted the entire steering committee about the lack of an editor. Two faculty volunteered to edit the self-study in a marathon weekend of writing and the document is submitted on time to the accreditation agency. As soon as the document is accepted, and before the site visit, Provost Kali fired Associate Provost Main. Although some detractors of the new president and Provost Kali spoke up about their feelings to the site visitors, the institution was reaccredited.

Questions

1. Should Provost Kali have replaced Associate Provost Main as soon as she was hired?
2. Should Provost Kali have reconstituted the self-study steering committee rather than working with the committee that was already in place?
3. Were there alternatives to firing the associate provost?
4. In general, how can a provost work to support the institution, and its president, when opinions around campus are deeply divided?

CASE 2: REORGANIZING THE PROVOST'S OFFICE

Provost White is new at a private institution. The past provost, Dr. Matter, served in that capacity for many years and depended heavily on his assistant, Ms. Origin. The provost has the associate provosts and other staff members in the office report directly to Ms. Origin, who has operated autocratically, giving orders without explanation and discouraging staff advancement.

The first week Provost White was in the office, the associate provost for student life and the associate provost for institutional research talked to him in private, asking to report directly to him instead of reporting to Ms. Origin. Their list of complaints was significant, ranging from lack of support for their professional development to negative comments in their evaluations without warning or justification. Provost White listened to their concerns, but chose to wait and observe, collecting solid facts before making a decision.

As time progressed, Provost White found that Ms. Origin was a very negative worker who did not favor the new provost's open and transparent style, his willingness to give everyone in the office an opportunity to express new ideas, and his support for positive change. Ms. Origin became more and more negative and staff meetings became a challenge. She opposed any new ideas that Provost White, the other associate provosts, or any of the other staff wanted to discuss much less to implement.

Ms. Origin also started sabotaging Provost White's requests, either by providing him with incorrect information and erroneous data or by simply not doing what she was asked to do. As a first step, Provost White had a serious conversation with Ms. Origin, who clearly expressed that she did not like the provost's leadership style, she was not willing to change, and she knew best because she had been running the office for many years.

Further meetings trying to resolve these issues resulted in no improvement in Ms. Origin's behavior. After consultation with the director of human resources, Provost White reorganized the office with all the associate provosts reporting directly to him rather than Ms. Origin, and upgraded two of the staff positions based on the evaluations of their duties. Ms. Origin continued as assistant to the provost but her duties were changed to technology manager.

Provost White hoped that this would improve the office environment, but unfortunately that was not the case and Ms. Origin became even more negative. She did not greet or interact with anyone else in the office and worked behind closed doors. Over the next five months, the office atmosphere continued to be very tense due to Ms. Origin's behavior.

After serious consideration of the situation, Provost White realized that Ms. Origin needed to be moved out of the provost's office. After further consultation with the HR director, Provost White spoke with Ms. Origin about moving her to another division.

This allowed Ms. Origin to refresh herself in a new environment without ties to her old division. The changes were shared in a staff meeting emphasizing the positive aspects of the shift and thanking Ms. Origin for her previous years of service.

Questions

1. Should Provost White have removed Ms. Origin at the beginning of his service?
2. How would you go about verifying the complaints of the associate provosts against a long-serving colleague?
3. What information do you have available for a viable solution?
4. Who could provide you with guidance in this situation?
5. If you want to relocate Ms. Origin, what steps do you need to take?
6. How would you approach a relocation conversation with Ms. Origin and the rest of the office staff?

Scenario 3

Provost Granteur is looking to fill a senior management position for his team. He has already carefully defined the skills and concrete work experience necessary for someone to succeed in the specific leadership position and has written a detailed job description. Provost Granteur's recruiting efforts have turned up a strong candidate whose skills and background seem to be a perfect fit for the job description. However, the provost is not quite sure how the candidate will fit with his team's culture.

Provost Granteur wants to identify options for assessing a candidate's cultural fit and reduce the risk of reliance on unconscious biases. He understands that determining whether a specific candidate is the right fit for his team's culture and work style can be challenging. Provost Granteur speaks with the president, a long-time friend and colleague.

The president provides Provost Granteur with some good ideas to ensure that the candidate will be a good cultural fit for the team. He suggests the provost ask the candidate to describe how he see the team's culture, how he sees his position as a senior manager, and to explain his personality and work style. Provost Granteur finds those suggestions worth following. Upon meeting again with the final candidate and asking those questions, the provost feels that the candidate will be a good fit for his team.

CASE 3: THE FIGHT OF THE PROVOST TO HIRE THE "RIGHT FIT" CANDIDATE

Provost Perez is fairly new at this comprehensive university. In all her trainings, Provost Perez has argued that culture fit is the most important aspect of retaining great employees, and can clearly articulate the aligned values, beliefs, behaviors, and experiences that make up her office's environment.

Provost Perez feels that defining her office culture, organization and values should be a priority in organizing her team at this new university because she is a firm believer that organizational culture needs to be decisively defined, nurtured, and protected.

So when Provost Perez is ready to hire an associate provost, she talked to the HR department to ensure that the job description clearly defined her office culture, strategic decisions, and strong commitment to clear and transparent communication. The HR director is reluctant to put what he considers "soft" skills in a hiring add.

Provost Perez explained to him that in her view "hiring employees that don't mesh well with the existing culture leads to poor work quality, decreased job satisfaction and a potentially toxic environment." She continued explaining: "This results in turnover and high cost to the university. On the other hand, hiring employees that fit well with the culture and share a strong belief in the values will most likely flourish."

The HR director challenges the provost, saying that looking for "fit" normally fails. He believes that a candidate should be hired based on subject matter expertise and a resume that fits perfectly with the job function the university is trying to fill. He goes on to tell the provost that in his many years as director of the HR department, he believes that after reviewing a resume, a successful phone screen and the first in-person interview, you are ready to hire the most competitive candidate before you lose them to another institution.

The Provost explains to him that just because you are afraid that a competitor school is going to beat you to the punch, you can't make rash hiring decisions without extensive analysis of whether that person is an ideal culture fit. Provost Perez states, "Getting this part wrong is very damaging to an institution, and that the new person won't stick around long anyway. Then it's back to the drawing board."

Provost Perez shares with the HR department director that she has made this mistake at her past institution, making terrible hires in key positions. The people had great resumes and they interviewed very well, but they didn't share the same values or vision for the university and were definitely not a culture fit.

She reassures the HR director that culture fit doesn't mean that an institution is recruiting the same kind of people with the same backgrounds and experiences. On the contrary, Provost Perez maintains, diversity is key to cultural fit. Provost Perez explains to the HR director the many ways to assess an individual's personality to see if they fit with the team environment.

She says, "You can take them on a tour of the office, let them sit in on a meeting or have them join you for a team lunch; in those situations it is easy to assess their comfort levels." And always ask for specific examples and experiences when you are posing a question.

Provost Perez finishes the conversation with the HR director, who still does not feel convinced about assessing cultural fit, by reminding him that hiring based on culture and values increases employee retention immensely. But it is not just about what is right for the university, it is also about what's best for the candidate. If you bring a candidate only for their expertise, knowing that they possibly are not the best culture fit, it is not fair to them. Provost Perez leaves the HR office hoping that she has stated her case well and that they will have a successful search.

The HR director spoke to the president about it because he wasn't convinced of the provost's arguments. The president, who has years of experience in higher education, agrees with the provost's viewpoints. They follow the provost's initiative on assessing cultural fitness, and end up hiring an associate provost that becomes a great team player and a future successor to the provost.

Questions

1. Do you agree with Dr. Perez's position?
2. Is cultural fit a necessary qualification for a job?
3. How would you assess cultural fit?
4. Is the HR director correct in challenging the provost?
5. What are your experiences with hires that fit or don't fit with the culture of your team?

FINAL THOUGHTS

Leaders come in two flavors, expanders and containers. The best leadership teams have a mix of both.

—Barbara Corcoran

An effective team can help your office achieve incredible results. On the other hand, a team that is not working can cause unnecessary disruption, failed delivery, and strategic failure. So, it's important for your success as a provost to know your team's strengths and weaknesses. This assessment will help you to uncover common team working problems that you might be experiencing. Once you have completed the assessment, you may want to look at tools that will help you to improve and develop your team in a positive way for success.

If you are hiring members for your team, the challenge is selecting the right person with the knowledge, skills, and ability to perform the job. However, not all hires are successful and a major reason is that the new employee is not a good fit for the team. In fact, the cost of hiring the wrong person can be high, not only financially but also emotionally in disturbing a working team. Fit is when there is a high degree of compatibility between the new team member's values and abilities and the team job requirements and values. Remember that it is very important that any person recruited onto your team should function effectively within your team culture.

You must look at the new team member's values. Values are the root of a person's personality and behavior. When the values of the team, the job, and the new candidate align, then positive outcomes are likely, including reduced turnover and increased job satisfaction, commitment to the office, and performance. Much can be learned about an applicant's values during an interview, but it requires a skilled interviewer who knows the office values as well as the desired characteristics, behaviors, and competencies needed to perform the job.

Individuals with a mismatch between their own values and the values of the job or the office likely will experience a lack of motivation and an inability to adapt to their work environment. A provost friend of ours suggests that when interviewing a new member for your office, you dig deeper to determine a person's core values, so you can determine whether this person is going to be a good fit for your team and the job to be performed.

Chapter 6

Collaborations across Other University Divisions

"First among Equals?"

This chapter deals with how the provost as the chief academic officer negotiates with the other divisions on campus to move the academic agenda along with the other divisions' priorities, emphasizing how to be "first among equals" to support the enterprise of the academy: the students.

The typical provost, as chief academic officer, is responsible for the largest division of the university and for its core mission, with the majority of the university's personnel and budget under the provost's direct supervision. At some universities, all or nearly all of the university reports to the provost, with the provost taking responsibility for day-to-day operations and the president focusing on strategic direction, philanthropy, and intercollegiate athletics.

At other universities, some or all of the functions not directly associated with the instructional mission report directly to the president, including IT, business affairs, EM, and student affairs.

When considering the individuals reporting directly to the president, position titles also are quite different from one university to another. At some institutions, the title of provost is considered to be separate from and superior to the vice presidential titles assigned to other presidential direct reports.

At other institutions, the provost has a more elevated vice presidential title than other vice presidents, so the provost might also be, for example, the only person with the rank of executive vice president. Finally, at still other institutions the provost might have the same vice presidential title assigned to the other major functions of the university, such as business affairs and student affairs.

With the additional titles, authority, and responsibilities of the provost varying significantly from one university to another, it is not unusual for new presidents to reorganize their universities and to add or take away supervisory responsibility from the provost. Each president has a different view of the role of the provost.

When a university changes presidents frequently, the position, power, and responsibility of the provost can increase or diminish with every new president. In the current era of constant electronic connectivity, the old expectation of the provost's authority—that provosts are in charge of the campus when the president is away—now means relatively little, as presidents today are easily able while traveling to provide timely direction about matters back on campus.

Further, longevity, experience, and already-existing relationships may give one or more individuals with direct reporting lines to the president the ability to exercise significant institutional influence, especially if these individuals have the trust of the president or key members of the BoT. In such cases, the perception, whether accurate or not, may be that one or more vice presidents other than the provost have more power than does the provost, even if formal institutional policy describes the provost as the "second-in-command."

These questions of power and influence are important because it is the long-standing custom in higher education that the provost, even if technically equal in title to other vice presidents, has the first and most important voice among those vice presidents. This custom, which is recognized in the written policies of some universities, is intended to clarify the chain of command when the president is away and to recognize the reality that the provost is responsible for the core institutional mission. However, as noted above, the understanding of the provost as "first among equals" is not honored at all universities.

Further, even when other vice presidents defer in one way or another to the special role played by the provost, the provost still is strongly advised to find ways to collaborate effectively with peer vice presidents. This chapter addresses several ways in which the work of the provost intersects with the efforts of those peers.

Scenario 1

When Dr. Zhung became a provost, she never felt "first among equals." She was the newest addition to the cabinet, the only female, the only minority, and perhaps the youngest at the time. There was another VP with many years of experience and a record of success who occupied the lead role. He was the president's right hand, and clearly the "first" among all the VPs. But Dr. Zhung did feel like an equal, and she tried hard to fit in her role as provost and advance the priorities of academic affairs.

Over time, the makeup of the cabinet changed and Dr. Zhung's role became more important in the cabinet. However, in her five years as provost she never felt "first." Therefore, when she became president at another university, she made sure that her provost was recognized as the most important VP in her cabinet and Dr. Zhung gave her provost added responsibilities.

CASE 1: HOW A NEW PROVOST BECAME "FIRST AMONG EQUALS"

Like most provosts, Dr. Jabbar had been a faculty member, having come up through the faculty ranks, only to discover that in his new role he was required not only to make judgments about his previous colleagues in terms of tenure and promotion but often to make difficult budgetary decisions, including potential layoffs of faculty and staff members alike. Some of his provost friends had also been promoted from within their institutions and found it difficult to say no to their friends and former colleagues.

One of Dr. Jabbar's colleagues at another university wanted to be loved more than respected, and she was appalled when she found herself easily vilified by those with whom she had previously been close.

As provost, Dr. Jabbar had read in multiple venues that he was "first among equals." But in his first weeks in the job he found himself sometimes at odds with his president and some of the other VPs because they didn't see how Dr. Jabbar's priorities were part of a larger institutional picture. Dr. Jabbar knew of provosts who had lost the confidence of their presidents, and in some instances their positions, because they were unwilling in times of financial shortfalls to recommend cuts in the academic budget.

As a new provost, Dr. Jabbar worked hard to make sure the other VPs saw him as an advocate for the faculty and the academic programs. At the same time, he supported and advocated for the decisions that the president and the board made, especially when those decisions were unpopular with the faculty. In addition, he worked hard to understand the abundance of decisions with which he was confronted on a daily basis, especially when he didn't have sufficient information or sufficient time for contemplation.

But Dr. Jabbar worked to be sure he was seen as "first among equals." After six months in the job, members of the cabinet started seeing him as an effective advocate in conversations with the president and respected his decisions as provost.

As Dr. Jabbar was reading an *Inside Higher Education* article illustrating the turmoil that a brief provost tenure can cause, he reflected on its message. He recognized the critical importance of effective academic leadership and the responsibility he had for the health, quality, and integrity of the academic programs, the faculty, the curriculum, the library, and the technology on his campus.

He believed that he took his role seriously, both the importance he had and the satisfaction that he derived from being in the number two position at the institution. This included being the "first among equals" within the senior administration and being the person in charge of the campus during presidential absences.

Dr. Jabbar truly appreciated the mentoring he had during his tenure as dean, understanding the importance of thinking institutionally and not just in terms of his own college, understanding the institution's mission and its strategic priorities, the budgeting process (including the major drivers in the budget) and the role deans play in the budgeting process. More than a decade ago, when Dr. Jabbar first became dean, he was typically given the opportunity to request additions to his college operating budgets.

As he was ending his dean's tenure, Dr. Jabbar often needed to make cuts rather than ask for new resources and to do so in the context of institutional rather than departmental needs and priorities. Dr. Jabbar was also privileged as dean to learn about the current state of admissions and retention, the ways that the institution integrated the curriculum and cocurricular programs, how student affairs provided support to the colleges, and information about fundraising goals, particularly those that related to the academic programs.

So as a new provost Dr. Jabbar felt he had the knowledge to do his job well. Furthermore, his president was absolutely clear about his expectations for the provost position and how he wanted to work with Dr. Jabbar as "first among equals." Because he was expected to raise money, he worked in collaboration with the VP for institutional advancement and accompanied her to cultivate and then solicit potential donors, whether individuals, foundations, or corporations.

Since he played a critical role in crafting the institutional budget, he collaborated with the VP for finance to unpack the budget and discuss its challenges. Dr. Jabbar also worked very closely with the VP for EM on admission and retention strategies including the financial aid discount, the institutional repositioning and the net tuition revenue. Another of his allies was the VP for student affairs as they worked together on opportunities and challenges on how student affairs and academic affairs were integrated.

By the end of his first year, working more closely with the other VPs and making it clear how the position of academic affairs was valued, made Dr. Jabbar "first among equals."

Questions

1. Have you read the book *First Among Equals*?
2. Do you feel that you as provost are the "first among equals" in your institution?

3. Do you agree with the strategies Dr. Jabbar used to get the respect and position of "first among equals" with the other VPs?
4. What other strategies would you use?
5. Do you think Dr. Jabbar's many years as dean have positioned him well for his new role?

Scenario 2

When Dr. Ramanashan was hired as provost at Merryweather University, he knew that he needed to work collaboratively with the other VPs. He also knew that his position was one of "first among equals." He was lucky that he understood budgets very well. He befriended the VP of finance and was able to negotiate funds for important academic programs very effectively.

The VP of finance was very happy to have for the first time a provost who understood budgets, spoke the language of the financial officer, and was able to collaborate in an intelligent manner. Dr. Ramanashan was always very supportive of what his fellow VPs wanted to do in their own divisions, very respectful of their areas, and sometimes was a coconspirator in achieving new initiatives on the campus. He felt that he was "first among equals," although sometimes the other VPs did not.

Dr. Ramanashan negotiated his salary to assure that it always would be higher than the other VPs, so he could perform his job as provost, promote academic affairs, and be the "first among equals."

Scenario 3

Provost Kwawe was hired at a public institution in the midst of a financial crisis. Provost Kwawe had never been a dean or other university officer, and her understanding of budget management was limited. Provost Kwawe was slow to ask for assistance and, from the perspective of the deans and other VPs, had a very convoluted way of sharing information or making requests.

The VP for finance, Mr. Price, tried to help Provost Kwawe, but she regularly appeared to ignore his advice and, in some cases, suggested that his advice was not welcome. The relationship between Provost Kwawe and Mr. Price became more and more strained over time. The tipping point was when Provost Kwawe authorized the hires of three faculty lines when she had been told by Mr. Price that, at the direction of the president, all hires for the year had been frozen.

This matter went all the way to the president, who had been feeling that he might have made a bad hire in Provost Kwawe. The president had full confidence in Mr. Price, who had navigated particularly bad economic times in a very efficient manner. The president had also been approached by the deans and the president of the university senate, all of whom were concerned about how difficult it was to work with Provost Kwawe.

They described her lack of clear communication in her requests. The president felt the time had come to let the provost go and he offered her a faculty position in the School of Education, but Provost Kwawe decided to leave the university. Her lessons learned included that understanding budgets and having a good relationship with the VP for finance are very important tools for success as a provost, especially in times of budgetary crises. She was more reluctant to recognize, however, that her approach to communication with faculty and administrators had also contributed to her ineffectiveness as provost.

Scenario 4

Provost Playoff had been provost at a private institution for over twenty years. For many years, he had been perceived as a weak provost, and as he aged his memory became impaired. Other VPs found it very difficult to work with him. They complained to the president, but the president wanted to leave Provost Playoff in his position until he was ready to retire.

Unfortunately, Provost Playoff offered the same $30,000 of the academic affairs budget to three different deans. When Dean Canae met with the VP of finance to get the money transferred to her college account, she found out that the provost had offered the same money to the other two deans, and that that money never existed in the academic affairs budget to begin with.

This was a tipping point for a situation that had been developing as Provost Playoff's memory was failing. Under the pressure of the VP of finance and the deans, the president offered Provost Playoff an early retirement package. The lesson learned: be aware of when it is time for you as a provost to leave the office before you are asked to leave.

Scenario 5

Provost Zsu played a key role in approving tenure bids and setting policies for academic hiring at his institution. His president and VP for enrollment were asking for changes on that policy, given their belief that the distribution of the tenured and tenure-track faculty was already inconsistent with present and future enrollment demand. Although Provost Zsu was open to change on some issues, he wasn't pushing for changes in the tenure process and the hiring of tenure-track positions.

Zsu felt that the provost's final decision on hiring and tenure was very important for his institution. Provost Zsu knew that some of his colleagues favored a system of increasing reliance on long-term faculty contracts over tenure-track appointments, while many of his peer institutions relied significantly on non-tenure-track professors. He did not want his institution to become more reliant on non-tenure-track faculty members and, therefore, he did not want to change the policies.

Because of pressure from his president, Provost Zsu offered the solution that, given the tight job market in many academic fields, the institution should reduce the number of students admitted to PhD programs, particularly those programs that have difficulty placing their graduates in good jobs. Provost Zsu tried to convince the VP of enrollment to see this as a viable approach that would create more flexibility in future faculty hiring. It was unclear to him that the president and the VP for enrollment would support his recommended action.

CASE 2: SPAN OF CONTROL ISSUES

One of the challenges of moving the academic priorities of the institution forward has to do with the structure of the Provost's portfolio. Each institution will have a different structure, and a provost who previously served at one institution as dean or other academic role may be surprised to find that her/his portfolio is very different at the next institution.

Provost Plumford had served as a dean at a medium-sized public institution and then moved on to become provost at a small private college, Colobus College. At Colobus, there were no deans—the provost was essentially dean of the faculty and had all department chairs reporting directly to her. At the same time, her portfolio included the registrar, academic advising, tutoring, career services, and the library. She was also delegated by the president to oversee the IT chief.

Thus, Provost Plumford had primary oversight of most all the units that would influence the recruitment, retention, and graduation of students. Her major points of negotiation with her cabinet colleagues had to do with student quality and numbers (with the VP for admissions) and student discipline and campus life (with the VP for student affairs).

Because she oversaw the majority of the staff who supported retention efforts, as well as having a direct line to the faculty through the department chairs, she was in a position to bring together most of the constituents who needed to be at the table to make major changes in retention rates, including bringing together technology, student academic support, and registration data to create a new retention plan. Some of her retention accomplishments played a direct role in her being recruited to a much larger private institution, Arabidopsis University.

Provost Plumford was surprised to discover that at Arabidopsis University her portfolio was much narrower than at Colobus. The registrar and career services at Arabidopsis reported to the VP for EM. Academic advising and tutoring reported to the VP for student affairs. The chief information officer reported to the CFO. Plumford's span of control included the deans, the library, and a few other faculty-facing units such as the grants administrator.

As a result, she faced a much more challenging political landscape when attempting to improve retention rates. It often seemed nearly impossible to even get a meeting at which all the relevant constituents could be present. She was saved by jumping on an opportunity to win grant money for Arabidopsis to participate in a national retention project funded by a prestigious foundation. The president at Arabidopsis was enthusiastic for the reputational gains that the institution would receive from winning the grant, which motivated the various VPs to send their people to meetings that Provost Plumford arranged in order to prepare the grant.

During the first year of the grant, Provost Plumford was usually able to get the players from other divisions to focus on the grant project and make some significant gains in retention for Arabidopsis University. However, as time went on the other VPs lost sight of the goal, and their direct reports frequently failed to show up for meetings or did not follow through on assignments. Provost Plumford finally decided that it was time to make a pitch to her president to reorganize the cabinet so that more of the academically related units would report to her.

Questions

1. What are the elements of the provost's portfolio at your institution? What are some of the pros and cons of the arrangement?
2. Provost Plumford's portfolio at Colobus resulted in her having as many as thirty-nine direct reports. How might this affect her ability to perform her duties?
3. What strategies, other than asking for a reorganization, might Provost Plumford try in order to keep the grant team functioning well?
4. What might the consequences be of Provost Plumford's request to her president for a reorganization for her relationships with the other VPs?

CASE 3: RALLYING AROUND AN OPPORTUNITY TO HELP STUDENTS

Provost Larchstein had a background in the natural sciences and had done quite a bit of grant writing during their time as a faculty member and as a dean. Larchstein was also in the vanguard of faculty who rejected traditional gender norms and was happy to have found in their new home, Darwin University (DU), an institution that embraced Larchstein's full identity, including their use of gender-neutral pronouns.

When they came to DU as provost, they discovered that DU had very little track record with institutional grant writing. They also discovered that there was a huge unmet need for student support. Faculty in the natural sciences had attempted to write grants that brought in funding to support stronger STEM curriculum and undergraduate research, but these attempts had been unsuccessful. These faculty approached Provost Larchstein about the possibility of their supporting the faculty efforts.

When Larchstein examined the previous grant attempts, they discovered that the faculty had not engaged with potential supporters across divisions of DU to put the grant project together. In fact, the faculty had not even engaged faculty from all the departments of the Division of Science, let alone the School of Education, where the curriculum change expertise was strong. Nonetheless, there were good ideas in the proposal and Provost Larchstein wanted to encourage the faculty to try again.

Provost Larchstein had one-on-one lunch meetings with their fellow VPs and asked for their support. They explained to the VP for enrollment that the grant, if funded, would provide much-needed scholarship money, and asked if someone from admissions could serve on a working group to rewrite and resubmit the grant. Enrollment was delighted to recommend someone. To the VP for student affairs, they explained that the close faculty mentoring proposed in the grant would be greatly helped if faculty could be paired with student affairs personnel who understood mentoring—this VP also recommended someone to join the grant writing effort.

Provost Larchstein was able, because the registrar and tutoring both reported to them, to assign some of their own staff to participate—but they made sure to have lunch with these colleagues as well, explain the purpose of the grant and the benefits to DU students if it should succeed.

The biggest hurdle to putting the new grant writing team together was with the VP of finance. While this VP was clearly eager to see more "soft money" flow into the university, she was reluctant to have someone from financial aid participate because these folks were "so very busy." Provost Larchstein, however, knew from their previous positions at other schools that the financial aid office was key to assuring that getting a grant-funded scholarship did not impair the ability of students to obtain the maximum state and federal aid to which they were entitled.

So, on a second meeting with the VP for finance, Larchstein did homework and brought some examples of how the grant would, if funded, not only bring "soft money" but also would likely increase net tuition revenue by improving recruitment and retention of STEM students. After that, the VP for finance was willing to send someone from financial aid to help write the grant.

When the new team was assembled, including the original faculty and some of their faculty colleagues from previously unrepresented departments, it took some time for Provost Larchstein to help them all get comfortable. Many faculty on the team had little experience dealing with the "back office" staff of DU and were not always respectful. The staff often resented the faculty for their "privileged" status and for the problems that they sometimes (albeit unwittingly) created for students by giving them bad advice about how to navigate the DU environment.

Provost Larchstein bought a lot of group lunches, made sure everyone had a chance to read the previous grants, and made sure there was plenty of time for everyone to speak up, share ideas, and participate in the process. Over time, as everyone became more comfortable, the group began to congeal around the goal of submitting a new version of the grant. Soon even some of the most reluctant faculty were enthusiastic.

The disappointment in the room was huge when the next round of grant awards was announced and DU was not among them. Provost Larchstein had their hands full keeping everyone from simply bailing out of the process. When the external reviews of the DU grant finally arrived, Larchstein called a meeting to share them. Before the meeting, Provost Larchstein read them thoroughly and placed a call to the officer at the granting agency that oversaw the program. Provost Larchstein realized that the agency was actually enthusiastic about DU's proposal—there were only a few items that needed work in order for it to be successful.

When the group met, Provost Larchstein read the reviews aloud and then shared the conversation with the grants officer. They urged the group to double down and do a rapid rewrite in order to meet the next possible deadline. On the next try, the agency funded DU's proposal for nearly $1 million. Following the announcement, Provost Larchstein invited the entire grant writing team, and all the VPs, to a party at their home to celebrate how the work of a strong team had succeeded.

Questions

1. Part of Larchstein's success was due to their background in the sciences, where grant writing is common. How might a provost from a non-STEM discipline learn to support such efforts?
2. Are there other units of the university that should have been included in the grant writing effort?
3. How can provosts work to break down barriers between faculty and staff in the absence of a group project such as this one?

4. What might Larchstein have done if one or more of the VPs were unwilling to have their unit participate in the project?

FINAL THOUGHTS

A leader takes people where they want to go. A great leader takes people where they don't necessarily want to go, but ought to be.

—Rosalynn Carter

Colleges and universities are living in an era of rapid and continuous change, so collaboration among the provost and the other VPs is a powerful vehicle to maximize institutional success. Collaboration requires individuals and institutions to step out of the comfort zones where they usually operate quite autonomously. To achieve the benefits that collaboration promises, the parties involved must learn how to work productively in tandem with others.

For example, work to improve retention routinely requires the collaboration of the VPs or other administrators who are responsible for the various functions away from the classroom that have consequences for student financial support and student well-being. No comprehensive retention plan can be implemented at the great majority of campuses without collaboration outside the academic affairs division.

There are several questions you may want to ask yourself to help working with your peer VPs. Why spend time and resources collaborating? What incentives motivate them to commit to collaboration? What challenges may be encountered along the way? One of the principal benefits of collaborating with others is to achieve goals that cannot be achieved alone. Also, collaborating with your peers can have other positive results, including more efficient sharing of resources, reductions in costs, and more coordinated efforts to facilitate student success.

Collaboration with your peers can unite you as allies against common rivals or to fight for a common cause. Institutions are seeking to learn about the newest or "best" practices in higher education. And new knowledge is best achieved by connecting with others and sharing information. Now, collaboration sometimes leads to conflict. The most common challenges of collaborating revolve around cultural differences, finding common interests and goals, time, geographic constraints, and power differences present in the group.

The relative balance (or imbalance) of power between peers is one of the factors that can most disrupt or complicate working collaborations. On the other hand, what makes collaboration with peers successful is trust, communication, a sense of shared interests and goals, and defined and clear expectations and roles.

In summary, each university takes a different approach to formalizing the authority of the provost, and other VPs will have diverse perspectives on the value of collaboration with the provost. The success of provosts at many universities depends to a significant degree on their ability to adapt to the unique situation at their institution and to manage relationships effectively with colleagues outside the academic affairs division. Just as with tenured faculty and established deans, the power to persuade usually is more central to the success of a provost than the ability to order or direct unilaterally that a change will be made or a new plan implemented.

Chapter 7

Supporting and Mentoring the Deans

"The Art of Delegation"

This chapter and the one following (chapter 8) recognize that deans lead their colleges or schools, but that the provost provides significant guidance in matters such as promotion and tenure, budgets, curriculum innovation, facility expansion, research initiatives, and program reviews. Strategizing with deans to optimize hires for growth, expansion, or faculty replacement will help the academic division to realize its goals. Most importantly, this chapter discusses when and what to delegate to deans, especially when difficult decisions need to be made.

Although a provost's primary duty is to be a visionary for the academic affairs unit of the university, a very important role of a provost is to support their deans, who are the visionaries of their colleges. At the same time, a provost needs to have confidence in the deans, so sometimes a provost has the difficult decision of removing a dean. The role of the provost in hiring new deans, whether to replace an existing dean or to found a new school or college within a university, is a key part of the job.

One of the best supports a provost can give a dean is to give them agency in setting and managing their budgets. This may mean that the whole university moves from a centralized budget system to a decentralized one, such as Responsibility-Centered Management (RCM), where college deans are completely responsible for their own budgets.

Or a provost may retain control but cede some decision-making powers to the deans depending on the nature of the institution and the position of the president and CFO. One of the downfalls of a decentralized system is that budgets are not pegged primarily to departmental enrollment but increasingly to tuition, with revenue generated by student credit hours.

That puts departments in competition with one another, sometimes duplicating efforts and courses. A provost's job is to help the deans, educating them about budget models such as zero-based budgeting, and supporting their decision-making as long as it is not detrimental to the university budget as a whole.

If you were unsure about what a provost does, you'll be perplexed at what many deans do anymore, particularly in institutions with decentralized budgeting. The reason for this is simple: when a growing number of provosts stopped advocating for faculty and balancing budgets in centralized systems, they typically lost focus or interest in the requisite duties of deans, especially since deans in decentralized systems often are responsible for revenue generation.

Deans are primarily responsible for emphasizing curricular-based experiences associated with EM, assessment, certification, curricular streamlining, nonduplication of pedagogy, as well as transparent student debt, retention, graduation rates, and job placement. Deans also need to advocate for the college, communicate well, collaborate, have vision, know budgeting, raise funds, promote diversity, understand shared governance, and support research. Deans, like provosts, need to be a jack-of-all-trades.

This is another area where seasoned provosts can mentor their deans. Some presidents have seen the problem with poorly defined roles for provosts and deans, and had to try to clarify them in order to help provosts mentor their deans.

Scenario 1

Provost Amichai arrived on his new campus as it was in the middle of an exciting construction project. After years of planning, the state had authorized a new building that would house departments spanning three of the schools—faculty from studio art, literature (both arts and sciences), computer science (engineering), and media arts (communications) would share a state-of-the-art facility designed to encourage them to collaborate across disciplines. Amichai was impressed with the architect's vision and was excited about the prospects for new academic programs that could arise.

A month after his arrival, however, the CFO called Amichai into her office and informed him that the project was seriously over budget. Due to construction problems with an elaborate fountain courtyard in the center of the building, the CFO told the provost that he needed to cut $2 million from the building budget.

Since the building was already well on its way to completion, that money would have to come from finishing items such as furniture and IT. Given the high-tech nature of the departments planned for the building, this news was disheartening to say the least. Amichai told the CFO that the deans and department chairs would be angry, and he worried that they would not cooperate. The CFO suggested that Amichai decide on the cuts himself.

Fortunately, Amichai knew that he did not have the necessary expertise to make these critical decisions on his own. His background was in mathematics, and he had no idea which of the hundreds of technical specifications and furnishings was most important to the success of the programs planned for the building. He therefore decided to bite the bullet, and he called a meeting of the three deans and the chairs of the affected departments.

Provost Amichai explained the situation and asked for their help in making wise choices. While the deans and chairs were, in fact, angry, they appreciated Amichai's openness and his willingness to involve them in making the budget decisions. After taking time to vent their frustrations, all of them dug in with the faculty in the affected departments and brought Amichai a list of changes that would help bring the project in on budget. The CFO was satisfied, and the building opened on time and to great fanfare.

Scenario 2

When Dr. Qadir became a provost, she understood the important role the deans play. Dr. Qadir wanted to create a cohesive dean team so she could delegate those responsibilities that were theirs to take. Dr. Qadir met with each dean individually on a regular basis, tried to address their concerns and requirements, and offer counsel where needed. She considered them the leaders of their own units, so she delegated the responsibility of decision-making that was directly related to their schools to them, and discouraged them from "kicking" the issue to the provost's office.

Dr. Qadir wanted the deans to feel empowered, and for decisions that impacted the academic affairs division, she wanted them to be part of a collaborative decision-making body. When conflicts arose, Dr. Qadir was lucky that usually there was relative agreement among the deans and the provost's office. Most often negotiations related to salary and other faculty benefits were issues, but Dr. Qadir had parameters and guidelines to follow.

Additionally, she was fortunate to have an associate provost who handled employee relations. He was quite skilled in working through faculty processes and handled all the frontline issues. To make more of a cohesive unit, Dr. Qadir involved the president in any controversial matters.

CASE 1: PROMOTING A CHAIR WITHOUT DEPARTMENTAL SUPPORT

Midtown University is a comprehensive institution, a unionized campus, and part of a state university system. The Department of Computer Science is a fairly new unit within the College of Arts and Sciences. Since its inception four years ago, its first chair, Professor Aniston, who announced a year ago that he would be retiring at the end of the fall, has led the department. In preparation for the transition, the department's assistant chair, Professor Leonardi, has been more and more heavily engaged in college-wide activities, with the understanding that she would step into the role as department chair upon Professor Aniston's departure.

The college dean, Dr. Samson, is also fairly new in her role. She has accepted the plan to move Dr. Leonardi into the role as department chair. As a result of Dr. Leonardi's expanded interaction within the college, Dean Samson and several other department chairs have noticed several facets of her personality that may not have been immediately apparent. She had a considerable ego, and never seems to tire of hearing her own voice.

Rather than taking time to observe and learn processes and protocols within the college, Dr. Leonardi has taken a strong leadership role, even before actually becoming department chair. In some instances, she has made commitments to faculty members within her department and throughout the college without having specific authorization to do so. While these behaviors have raised eyebrows in some corners, the process of transitioning from Prof. Aniston to Dr. Leonardi has continued apace.

In the past week, Dean Samson has been given some disturbing new information. It appears that Dr. Leonardi has recently adopted positions and expectations directly contradicting those of her immediate supervisor, Prof. Aniston. This has led to increasing uncertainty and confusion within the department and across the college regarding the policies and goals of the Department of Computer Science.

Even more worrisome, Dean Samson has learned that Dr. Leonardi has been verbally and emotionally abusive to departmental staff members, in some cases reducing office administrators to tears. Dean Samson decides to consult with her provost about how to proceed. Provost Rejnish has been in his position for many years and has a very good grasp of university policies and working within union constraints.

Provost Rejnish convinced the dean to reverse her decision to appoint Leonardi and encourage her to do a national search for a new chair. Dr. Leonardi is furious when the dean breaks the news to her and immediately seeks union advice to grieve the dean and the provost.

Questions

1. What options are available to Dean Samson and Provost Rejnish at this point? What would be the advantages/disadvantages of each of these options?

2. What might Dean Samson and Provost Rejnish have done previously to avoid arriving at this point?
3. Does this situation raise the possibility of gender bias? Is Dr. Leonardi being unfairly judged because of her gender?
4. How can the dean and the provost work together to resolve the grievance?

Scenario 3

When Dr. Sabra was a dean, she had a very aloof and nonengaging provost. She knew that when she became provost, it was her job to mentor her deans, not only on their jobs but also to prepare them to move up in the senior administration track. Dr. Sabra knew when to delegate to the deans, but also to be available to them if needed.

Dr. Sabra met regularly with her dean's council to discuss actions the deans wanted to take so that neither the deans nor the provost would get in trouble. Dr. Sabra also saw her job as protecting her deans from the president and taking the responsibility for decision-making.

Scenario 4

Dr. Red was the first minority dean and the only female appointed to such position in a small private university. Provost Rowel had felt the pressure from his president to hire a minority dean to diversify the upper administration at the institution. Dr. Red had plenty of experience as a department chair, associate provost, and associate dean. In all of those positions, she felt handicapped because of being a minority.

Unfortunately, Provost Rowel didn't make her feel any different. At deans' council, he never listened to Dr. Red's ideas and found her unprofessional because of her mannerisms. Dr. Red wrote a white paper about the need for a new core in her school and the faculty union president, who has been at the institution in that capacity for thirty-five years, wrote a disparaging letter about the dean and her ridiculous idea of revising the core.

Provost Rowel asked Dean Red to retrieve the white paper and apologize to the faculty union president. Dr. Red was livid. She had spent a year consulting with faculty in her college about what major changes were needed. She felt that the provost should be supporting her and not the faculty union president who was very recalcitrant about any change.

Provost Rowel called Dr. Red at home on a Sunday night to tell her he was expecting an apology the next day, and so was the president. That Monday, Dr. Red made an appointment with the president, who was totally unaware of the situation. The president had been trying to move the university forward and was also having problems with the faculty union president and his unwillingness to make changes.

The president called Provost Rowel to the office and praised Dr. Red for her initiative and asked the provost to support Dr. Red. This did not set well with the provost, and during the remaining two years of his tenure, he and Dr. Red had a very confrontational relationship. When Provost Rowel retired and a new provost was hired, things changed for Dr. Red.

The new provost was very supportive of her deans; she was also a female and a change agent. Dr. Red and the new provost worked together in changing the core, and after four years of hard work the new core was approved and passed, against the faculty union president's resistance, with full support from the faculty. Dr. Red understood that a good provost supports her deans within reason, and empowers them to make the changes necessary in their colleges.

CASE 2: A PROVOST'S HASTY CHANGES OF A DEANS' COUNCIL

Dr. Hunt was hired as a provost at Glenwood University, a public university growing in its research agenda to become an R-1 institution. The university has six colleges with six deans that had been hired by the past or current president. Dr. Hunt felt that none of the deans were suited to move the university forward on the research front. He thought, and decided, that he needed to reshape his dean's team.

He first fired the dean of fine and performing arts, a dean that had been serving for more than twenty years and had been interim provost for three of those years. He fired him on grounds of lack of knowledge in the field of research in the arts. He then fired the dean of business on grounds of mismanagement of funds in the college. The next dean to be fired was the dean of communication because of a disagreement they had about a tenure case in the college.

Provost Hunt then also fired the dean of engineering using faulty accusations against that dean that were provided by faculty in his college. The next to go was the dean of liberal arts and sciences on grounds of poor performance and lack of supervision of the college budget. Dr. Hunt's last dean to be fired was the dean of education, in spite of the fact that she was the protégée of the chief of staff. This created a rift between the chief of staff and the provost.

All this happened in less than two years. There was a serious concern by the faculty and the other vice presidents about Provost Hunt's reshaping of his dean's team. The main concern was that Provost Hunt not only was firing the prior deans without much cause, but he was surrounding himself with new "yes" deans to move his agenda forward in a speedy way that faculty were not ready for or aware of. The president was silent, and let Provost Hunt manage his new deans' appointments as he wished, although he was aware of the concerns of the faculty, the other vice presidents, and in particular the chief of staff.

This rapid change of senior management at the college level brought many faculty concerns and a climate of unrest and insecurity. Provost Hunt wasn't impacted by the poor climate among the faculty ranks or the lack of support from them or the other vice presidents. He surrounded himself with a new dean's council that obeyed his orders, firing or denying tenure to faculty that didn't move their agenda to high levels of research with substantial grant awards.

Questions

1. Do you think Provost Hunt acted in a hasty manner?
2. Was he just following his goal to make Glenwood University a highly rated R-1 University?
3. How would you prepare as provost for a major change in campus philosophy?
4. How would you have handled the situation if you were in Provost Hunt's position?

CASE 3: FOLLOWING THE ADVICE OF A DEAN MAY NOT BE THE BEST IDEA

At a small liberal arts institution, Dr. Muhad, the dean of the School of Liberal Arts and Sciences, is going to retire at the end of the academic year. Dr. Muhad has been the provost's most trusted dean and a close friend and had been a dean for many years when Provost Jafari was hired. Since Provost Jafari came to the provost's position from being the dean of liberal arts and sciences, the connection with Dean Muhad was immediate.

The college was like many small liberal arts institutions with serious economic problems, and Provost Jafari was concerned about the expense of hiring a consulting firm to manage the search to replace Dr. Muhad. In a conversation between the dean and the provost, Dr. Muhad suggested that the associate dean, Dr. Johnson, would be a good replacement.

Dr. Johnson was an excellent associate dean, highly responsible, and also had a long history in the school since he came from its faculty ranks. Dr. Johnson had great rapport with the chairs in the school and the faculty saw the move as fair. Dr. Muhad had nothing but positive things to say about Dr. Johnson. Provost Jafari liked the idea, especially because it was a recommendation of Dean Muhad and because it would save the college money.

The provost consulted with the president about naming Dr. Johnson the dean of the School of Liberal Arts and Sciences once Dean Muhad retired.

The president agreed with the decision. Provost Jafari also consulted with the senior faculty of the school and got very positive feedback about naming Dr. Johnson. Dean Muhad was very pleased since she thought her successor was an excellent choice for the school. A year after Dr. Muhad retired, she went back to the institution for reunion weekend.

To her surprise, Provost Jafari was very unhappy with the performance of Dean Johnson. He had become a troublemaker on the dean's council and bypassed the provost many times to work directly with the president or the other vice presidents to get things for the school.

When Dr. Muhad talked with the staff and faculty in the school, she heard similar stories. Dr. Johnson was a micromanager, made decisions without faculty consultation, did not involve his staff in what was going on at the college level, and had antagonized many of the departmental chairs. Dr. Muhad felt badly about the outcome and she and the provost were trying to figure out what went wrong, including how Dean Johnson's personality had changed so much.

Questions

1. Was Provost Jafari right in taking advice from Dean Muhad?
2. Why do you think Dr. Johnson became such a poor choice as a dean?
3. If you were the provost, what next steps would you take regarding Dean Johnson?
4. Do you think that power changes people?
5. How can we forecast someone's behavior before promoting him or her?

CASE 4: THE DUELING DEANS

For three decades, the Department of Communication Studies at a large comprehensive university has been housed in the College of Liberal Arts. Over half the department's major enrollments are in its concentration in public relations. The major has been "certified" as part of a quality assurance process administered by a well-regarded international professional association that does not accredit programs.

Simultaneously, a growing College of Mass Communications now is responsible for nearly 10 percent of enrollments at the university, and an international professional association accredits the mass communications degree programs. Because of conflicts in earlier years, the communication studies faculty and the mass communications faculty rarely interact, and the members of those faculties usually maintain that they represent separate disciplines.

When the newly appointed Provost Gladestone arrived on campus, following a search in which Gladestone received unanimous support from all campus constituencies, the provost scheduled a first round of meetings with the deans. Provost Gladestone soon learned that there was a serious conflict involving the public relations concentration. Dean Cross, of the College of Mass Communications, maintained that public relations is a professional program that should be located in the College of Mass Communications, as it most typically is at other large universities.

Dean Cross believed students would benefit from receiving their degrees in a professionally accredited College of Mass Communications. Dean Molestando, of the College of Liberal Arts, maintained that the public relations concentration had been successfully offered for decades to a large number of students in the Department of Communication Studies, with evidence of student satisfaction and strong job placement for new graduates. Dean Molestando stated that there was no need to relocate a successful program, for which many departmental faculty had been recruited over the years.

Five years earlier, a lengthy task force report recommended the public relations concentration be moved to the College of Mass Communication, by a split vote of 7-5. A month after the task force report was issued, the American Association of University Professors (AAUP) chapter at this nonunion campus unanimously endorsed a motion stating that no academic programs or faculty should be relocated from one college to another without the unanimous agreement of the affected faculty. No action was taken as a result of the task force report because of the AAUP motion.

Two years following the appearance of the task force report and after a shouting match over this subject at a faculty senate meeting, the retiring provost stated that the next provost would need to resolve this matter, as it would be unfair for a provost with no long-term commitment to do so.

The interim provost, who served for two years after the provost's retirement, also believed this conflict should only be resolved by a permanent provost. Meanwhile, for years the faculty of the Department of Communication Studies had offered criticisms of the quality of the programs and faculty of the College of Mass Communications, and the other faculty had reciprocated their behavior.

This conflict has now been unresolved for over a half-decade. Deans Cross and Molestando avoid each other whenever they can. Both deans already have secured letters of support from students, alumni, and community leaders for their respective positions. Both deans are relatively new, are protective of their programs, and seem reluctant to compromise and unlikely to leave the university. Dean Cross has indicated that mass communications faculty intend to bring this matter to the faculty senate and to the board of regents if the matter is not resolved in the current academic year.

Dean Molestando suggested that two significant donors to the College of Liberal Arts are public relations graduates who would be upset if their program is relocated. The current faculty senate president is a mass communications faculty member who supports program relocation. A public relations alumnus and personal friend of Dean Cross is the vice chair of the BoT. Dean Molestando informed Provost Gladestone that early discussions with a major donor over a naming gift for the College of Mass Communications had included questions about the location of the public relations program.

The university's president had a nonacademic career in business and politics, and his relationship with the faculty was damaged in the past few months because of an athletics controversy. The president told Provost Gladestone that the academic leadership must ultimately solve this academic dispute during the next year—in a way that does not upset the BoT or the campus community—while being mindful of the university's current budget shortfall.

The provost believed the president did not want a political fuss, and the president wanted Provost Gladestone to know that the university could not afford to buy off whichever dean did not get his or her way. The president admitted to Provost Gladestone that this public relations concentration dispute was a "problem from hell" and would be the first significant challenge to Provost Gladestone's leadership on campus.

By university policy, the provost has the sole authority to reorganize academic departments and to assign degree programs and faculty to the appropriate college, though there is an inconsistently applied tradition at the university of advisory votes by the faculty senate and by the deans on major academic reorganizations.

A week after Provost Gladestone's conversation with the president, a student reporter requested an interview with the provost about "the ongoing problems with the faculty and quality of the unaccredited public relations program." It was now the fifth week of Provost Gladestone's first semester at her new job.

Provost Gladestone sent a short statement of support for the public relations program to the student reporter and declined the interview. The provost then scheduled individual meetings with each tenured full professor in the two academic units. She also called a joint meeting of the faculties, chairs, and deans for the College of Mass Communications and the Department of Communication Studies, in which she indicated that she was new to the campus, had an open mind, and wanted to hear what they had to say about the matter, no matter how long the meeting lasted. The provost also met with the alumni and community advisory boards for both units.

After hearing from all parties, the provost announced that a new task force, to be appointed by the provost and made up primarily of communication studies and mass communications faculty from other highly regarded universities and by outside professionals, which would review the matter and make a recommendation to the provost by March 1. After providing all parties the time to comment in writing on the task force recommendation, the provost would consult with the president and announce a final and binding decision about the task force recommendation.

The task force was appointed and adopted an inclusive approach to gathering information, though not all faculty were pleased with the task force membership. The task force recommended, by a 5-2 vote, that the public relations concentration and its faculty should be moved to the College of Mass Communications, and the provost accepted the recommendation, with the move to take effect following a two-year transition period. The president praised the task force for its hard work and the provost for her commitment to a fair process, while declining to express an opinion about what he considered a matter of academic administration.

Two faculty announced that they were leaving the university because of the decision to relocate the program, though only one of the two did so. The AAUP chapter unanimously adopted a motion calling for a new procedure in which, in the future, a favorable faculty senate vote would be required to relocate an academic program, but the administration declined to make this policy change. For the next three years, about a third of the tenured faculty in the College of Liberal Arts gave Provost Gladestone a rating of "unsatisfactory" in their anonymous individual reviews of her performance.

The provost was cross-examined at length about the relocation decision in an hour-long executive session of the board of regents. One regent stated that this decision had caused him to permanently lose respect for the provost's judgment. Other regents said they accepted and understood the provost's decision.

Two years later, when the president retired, one of the deans was asked to serve as interim president. It was credibly reported on campus that the regents had not offered the interim presidency to the provost in part because a few regents still questioned her handling of the public relations conflict.

Following the relocation decision, two donors quietly indicated that they would not be making future gifts to the College. However, a very large naming gift eventually was made for the College of Mass Communications, with the donor publicly thanking Provost Gladestone for her leadership in bringing the public relations concentration to the "right college." The grateful donor set aside a specific gift to endow some of the operating expenses of the public relations program.

Questions

1. The provost has the advantage of being new to this dispute. How might newcomer status be an advantage in resolving this matter?
2. Which dean has the better case for her or his position?
3. Separate from the merits of the program's location in one college or another, what are the great challenges in managing the power dynamics and personalities in this conflict?
4. What would you do to move toward a final resolution of this dispute?

FINAL THOUGHTS

The best leader is the one who has sense enough to pick good people to do what he wants done, and self-restraint enough to keep from meddling with them while they do it.

—Theodore Roosevelt

As provost, you are in charge of all academic affairs at the university and your best allies in helping with your job are your deans. When working with your deans, the areas that will probably generate the most conflict will be budget allocation and budget cuts. In general, the office of provost no longer is chiefly responsible for budget (centralized system); instead, college deans are responsible (decentralized system).

That puts deans in competition with one another. In general, the new class of deans typically haven't a clue about accounting. As a provost you can help your deans by offering budget education, especially if your institution has an RCM model. Another best way to help your deans is creating a culture of collaboration among them, and with you. Nothing works better that a group of deans that communicate well, collaborate with each other, have a common vision, raise funds together for the good of the university, promote diversity, promote student success, and are advocates of shared governance.

In our opinion, higher education cannot continue to thrive without a strong provost that supports the deans in their endeavors.

Chapter 8

Provost and Dean in Faculty Issues

This chapter includes case studies on how provosts negotiate with their deans when dealing with faculty issues. Supporting faculty will promote engaged and productive departments. Promoting faculty growth and development and rewarding faculty through recognition shows respect and will make faculty feel that their contributions to the university are valued. Navigating the roles of the provost versus the dean in dealing with faculty is sometimes a blurred and dangerous line. Some of the cases and personal stories reflect on the leading strategies in this area.

In US higher education, the usual chain of supervision begins with faculty reporting to department chairs or program directors, who then report to deans. Deans are in turn reporting to provosts, who themselves report to presidents or chancellors.

In chapter 7, we talked about the role of the provost in supporting and mentoring deans and the challenges that come when deans disagree with one another. In the current chapter, we focus specifically on cases and scenarios that concern faculty issues, including hiring, tenure, promotion, and departmental supervision. Because faculty unions create very different management challenges and opportunities when compared with nonunion campuses, unions get some coverage here.

In reviewing these cases and scenarios, it is helpful to remember that some universities are far more decentralized than others in making personnel decisions. In some institutions, faculty, chairs, and deans have considerable independence in managing their own personnel budgets, in hiring and firing faculty, and in selecting department chairs and program directors. As a practical matter, the provost rarely scrutinizes even tenure and promotion decisions at decentralized institutions.

In contrast, the provosts at more centralized (and, often, relatively small) institutions may be heavily involved in hiring and personnel decisions. Chapter 7 provides additional discussion of the effects of decentralization on the relationship between provosts and deans.

CASE 1: A TENURE DENIAL

Provost Chin has been hired to increase the research visibility of a comprehensive private university. Recently, he hired Dr. Mytical to be Dean of the College of Arts and Sciences. Mytical comes with a strong track record as a faculty member and department chair at a research intensive institution, and Provost Chin believes she will help to stimulate more research activity.

It is faculty promotion and tenure season, and the Department of Political Sciences Promotion and Tenure Committee, a body composed of all tenured faculty members, has voted to deny promotion and tenure to Dr. Stym. Dr. Stym has a stellar record as a teacher, particularly in the large enrollment sections of Introduction to Political Sciences. Her service record is satisfactory for a junior faculty member.

The committee vote was close (5-3) and was largely based on strong disagreements about Stym's research. Although the number of articles published during her probationary period met the departmental criteria for promotion and tenure, some committee members argue that her coauthored publications should not count because she played a secondary role that was not significant. In addition, they take issue with the fact that two of her first-authored publications are in political science education, rather than her specialty area within the discipline. The latter publications resulted from an NSF CCLI[1] grant on which she was the PI.

Although the committee's deliberations are intended to be confidential, word quickly leaks to the dean and the provost. Just six months into her tenure as dean, Dr. Mytical felt she was in a difficult situation. Citing the fact that her prior annual reviews have been positive, Dr. Stym has decided to appeal the tenure and promotion denial to the dean. As someone who was recruited from a research university, Dr. Mytical has not yet garnered a sense of her institution's expectations for advancement, but her own assessment was that Dr. Stym met the criteria as specified in the department's evaluation policy.

However, she finds the prospect of overturning the majority vote of her colleagues to be a daunting one, as she is new to a leadership role and actively establishing her credibility in the position. She knows the political science

---

[1] National Science Foundation Course; Curriculum and Laboratory Improvement, respectively.

department has had a spotty record with regard to recruiting and retaining female faculty members.

Since promotion and tenure decisions rest with the Provost, Dr. Mytical calls for a meeting with Provost Chin. The meeting does not go well, since Provost Chin does not want to give tenure and promotion to Dr. Stym. Clearly, the dean and the provost are not on the same page, and Provost Chin does not want to delegate the final authority to her dean.

Questions

1. How can the dean and the provost negotiate this case?
2. Is there evidence that the committee is applying the criteria for advancement inappropriately? If so, what can the dean and provost do?
3. What strategies might Dean Mytical utilize in responding to the appeal that are mindful of her need to establish credibility?
4. What steps might Provost Chin take to mitigate the negative impact of overturning her dean?

Scenario 1

As provost at a large university, Dr. Rashid tried to be very respectful of his deans when it came to faculty issues. If a faculty member called or showed up in his office, Dr. Rashid would listen to them, but let the dean know immediately, and never did an end-run on a dean. Dr. Rashid felt that it was very important to have a healthy and functioning dean team. In times when Dr. Rashid needed to make recommendations different from those of a dean, he always talked to the dean prior to taking his actions to the president.

Overall, Dr. Rashid always felt that he had a very constructive team that was open to new ideas and discussions of problems in the different colleges, and worked together to solve difficult problems. Dr. Rashid was always a firm believer on supporting his deans and, unless necessary, let them be the "presidents" of their colleges.

CASE 2: A PROVOST DECISION ON A FACULTY SEARCH

A few years before Dr. Shaurya was named provost, a faculty member in the philosophy department had been denied tenure by the administration and the department had been furious. The candidate's publication record was paltry and included "in press" publications in edited volumes that were on the curriculum vitae year after year, showing no signs of becoming published.

A couple of years later, when Dr. Shaurya was in office as provost, the wife of a promising young faculty member in the mathematics department applied for a position in philosophy. Rumors flowed that the mathematician would leave if his wife did not get the position in philosophy. Provost Shaurya very much wanted to keep the mathematician and hoped that the search committee in philosophy would recommend the wife, but she avoided intervening in the search process. It was important that the search committee carry out its work independent of any outside influence.

The chair and the senior member of the philosophy department asked to meet with Provost Shaurya about the search. She wisely asked their dean to join the meeting because he was the dean of their division and nothing should be said about the search that he did not hear. Provost Shaurya was also wary of what might be said in the meeting and she wanted a witness.

The chair had been embittered by his inability to gain promotion to full professor having never published; he believed that the expectations for promotion had changed over time, a situation he deemed unfair. The senior member of the department was a highly published scholar who had graduated from one of the most esteemed universities in the English-speaking world, but who had established himself as the antagonist of the administration on nearly every issue, even those in which he had no personal interest.

A meeting occurred in Provost Shaurya's office that included all members of the search committee of the philosophy department as well as the dean. One of the faculty on the philosophy department search committee made the observation that the college wanted to keep the mathematician. It quickly became clear that the search committee were offering a quid pro quo. They would select the wife in the search, thus allowing the college to keep the mathematician, if Provost Shaurya reversed the administration decision on the philosopher who had been denied tenure previously and bring him back.

Upon realizing what they were offering, Provost Shaurya reiterated what she believed they were saying and indicated that she did not make deals in her office. She suggested that they end the meeting. The philosophy search committee continued to press for the deal, becoming more agitated that Provost Shaurya was unwilling to engage in the discussion. "You make deals here all the time," claimed the senior member.

Keeping her composure, Provost Shaurya said that the meeting was over, stood up, and started walking toward the door to open it. The senior member then stood up and blocked her way to the door. He said, "The meeting is *not* over." Provost Shaurya and the senior faculty would have been nose-to-nose but he stood quite a few inches taller than she, so they were more nose-to-neck. Provost Shaurya looked up and said calmly, "I would hate to have to call security." The chair, still seated, said, "Please, no."

The senior member stepped away, Provost Shaurya moved to the door, opened it, and stood beside it waiting for them to leave. As the senior member approached the open door, he said, "This is the last time I cooperate with this administration," which was humorous because he had never cooperated with the administration.

After the search committee members left, the dean and the provost expressed their amazement over the interaction—their interest in making such a deal, the senior member's blocking the provost's way, and his aggressive comment as he left, not to mention the irony given that the senior member's modus operandi was to continually try to paint the administration as being corrupt.

The senior member called several hours later to apologize. No deal was ever made. Ultimately, the philosophy search committee recommended the mathematician's wife, she joined the faculty, and there they both remain years later.

Questions

1. Was Provost Shaurya correct in inviting the dean to the meeting?
2. Would you have denied the deal as provost Shaurya did? Why, or why not?
3. What should Provost Shaurya and the dean have done about the recalcitrant senior member in the department?
4. How might the meeting have been different had the provost not invited the dean to attend?
5. Do you think the search ended in a good way? Why or why not?

CASE 3: AN UNTENURED FACULTY INTERACTS WITH THE PROVOST

Dr. Renata was an untenured faculty member in a teacher education department when she interacted with Provost Fuelling. Soon after Dr. Renata's appointment, the Dean offered her the opportunity to make some extra money by observing instructors teaching in an off-campus program. Working with the teachers' union, the college was offering graduate courses—courses that met the foundational requirements for the master's degree the university offered—at school sites.

When Dr. Renata came to observe, it was clear that the curriculum of the courses was not only completely different from the on-campus courses, it was also not appropriate. The course had no merit and it was gimmicky, with poor content that had no research base and was not accepted within the discipline.

The teacher's union was hiring its leaders as the teachers, allowing them to be paid as college adjuncts. The whole program existed to make money for the college and had no academic merit whatsoever. Consequently, Dr. Renata declined to do any more observations.

After that, Dr. Renata began to see that practicing teachers, after completing as many as three courses (out of thirteen required courses) in the off-campus program, were coming to campus to complete their master's degrees—lacking the true content of the three courses. Or they were transferring these courses to other colleges which had no way of knowing that the content had not been the one described in the college catalog.

Despite her untenured status, Dr. Renata began to speak up in department meetings against the off-campus program, which shook up the dean, who had brokered this arrangement with the teachers' union. The department chair could not ignore Dr. Renata's observations because they had to do with the academic quality of one of the department's programs, so he pushed the matter off to the provost, bypassing the dean. Provost Fuelling called Dr. Renata into his office.

Dr. Renata had only met the provost once, at the time she was being interviewed for the job. The provost claimed to be surprised at Dr. Renata's assertions that the off-campus program lacked academic merit, but Dr. Renata explained why this was true. The provost tried to convince her otherwise, but it was Dr. Renata's field, not his, so Provost Fuelling had no academic background in the matter. He offered Dr. Renata the opportunity to revise the curriculum for extra pay; she declined. The provost said he would have to look into it, speak with the dean, and get back to her.

It was only after this meeting that Dr. Renata realized how much she had risked in making an issue of the off-campus program's content. She was an untenured faculty member who was, in effect, denying the provost a regular source of considerable revenue for the college.

Dr. Renata decided to approach the problem in stages. First, she suggested to her department chair that they count the courses as electives instead of required courses in the program. He happily agreed to that. This way, the college continued to make the money it was used to receiving, but the courses could not count as the foundational required courses.

Dr. Renata's second stage required the assistance of a colleague. The program had three faculty members: the department chair, who had worked with the dean to establish the off-campus program with the teachers' union, Dr. Renata, and one other faculty member. Dr. Renata used the following year to convince the other faculty member that they should give these off-campus programs unique course numbers and that *they would not count toward their program at all*, not even as electives. Dr. Renata had the votes. To the chagrin of the dean and the provost, she had gotten these courses out of their program.

Once the courses were not counted toward anything, the teachers' union decided to move the off-campus program to a college that would count the courses toward a degree, and broke off their arrangement with Dr. Renata's college. The dean and the provost never forgave Dr. Renata. Provost Fuelling would not make eye contact with her, and the dean wanted to deny her tenure. To Dr. Renata's luck, both the dean and the provost were soon let go when a new president was appointed. After a six-year period, Dr. Renata was granted tenure.

Questions

1. Was Provost Fuelling appropriate in meeting with Dr. Renata without the dean?
2. Was Dr. Renata right in her quest?
3. Do you think that if the dean and the provost were not removed, would Dr. Renata have ever gotten tenure?
4. If you were Provost Fuelling, how would you have handled the matter?

Scenario 2

Concerns suggesting bias in the reviews students give their professors have been arriving at Provost Mombawe's desk with increasing frequency. Provost Mombawe knew that student evaluations of professors were important to the careers of faculty members.

Provost Mombawe's institution used student evaluations when judging faculty members for tenure, promotion, or raises. In terms of the significance of the evaluations, her institution considered student reviews very important. But Provost Mombawe was concerned about the validity of the evaluations, especially that they may not be accurate or may result in unfair criticism of female or minority faculty members. Provost Mombawe requested that the university senate work on restructuring student evaluations and reconsider how they are used in reviews of professors for tenure, promotion, or merit raises.

Scenario 3

The Department of Mathematics at Small Private College (SPC) has had some retirements, and as one of the major service departments, it desperately needs to increase its ranks. Provost Palmyra approves a search. The department and the dean interview candidates and recommend a hire to the provost. The provost reviews the file on the potential hire, who has taught at SPC as an adjunct, and notes that the candidate's teaching evaluations are weak.

Questioning the dean, Provost Palmyra learns that the chair of the department, a long-standing power broker on campus, has a personal relationship with the candidate and has been strongly advocating for the hire. The dean is reluctant to deny the hire because of the chair's political clout—she is concerned that he will retaliate in ways that will make it impossible to work with other faculty.

Provost Palmyra decides to meet all the finalists herself, and discovers that the favored candidate, while a brilliant scholar, has very poor communication skills that are unlikely to make him an effective teacher. Rather than tell the department and dean that they must hire one of the other candidates, Provost Palmyra tells the dean that the department may not hire their favorite candidate, but has the option of either making an offer to any one of the others or extending the search and looking for additional candidates.

Scenario 4

Working with a faculty union can be challenging for any provost. When Provost Carolina was hired at a small college, she found herself dealing with a union issue. The issue had to do with a faculty member notifying the administration of an anticipated spousal surgery and the need to take care-giving time, use of sick time, and overload payment.

The faculty member gave the dean less than twenty-four-hour notice that his spouse was having major surgery. The faculty member was helping his chair hire an adjunct faculty member for his several weeks anticipated absence for one course, and for another course he planned to do alternate assignments and come in some of the time. He planned to use sick days to cover the remaining days that he would miss.

He was scheduled for an overload assignment—in union parlance this is workload above usual—for which additional payment is provided. Given this scenario and the inability for the faculty member to actually work overload, the dean recommended changing the faculty member to normal workload. The faculty member had had the overload assignment for several years and so had come to see it as salary, so this became a grievance against the dean and was supported by the union.

The union president was very strong in advocating for the faculty member to get to keep the overload, despite the need to hire someone to cover the absence. In private, he was also willing to acknowledge that the faculty member's last-minute notification and nonspecific plan for meeting the students' needs in the other course via alternate assignment were not optimal. Human resources had a significant concern about the use of sick time to partially cover what should have been family medical leave.

The key was working out an overall solution between the school, the provost's office, the faculty union, and human resources. Ultimately, deciding to allow the faculty member to retain overload allowed for a union contract addendum spelling out how sick time could and could not be used, required notification regarding a planned absence, and use of overload going forward.

CASE 4: LISTENING TO ONLY ONE VERSION OF A PROBLEM

At a large public research university, Provost Verdibo has been in the job for over six years. He rose through the ranks within the university. One day Provost Verdibo received a visit from three senior faculty from the Department of Dysfunctional Science, complaining about their chair, Dr. Swim. Their claim is that she has been harassing the members of the department, has fired a secretary without reason, and biases the younger faculty against the senior ones. Two of the senior faculty members are personal friends of Provost Verdibo.

The provost, without any investigation of the claims and without checking with the dean of the College of the Sciences, decides to remove the chair from her position, take away her sabbatical and research release time, and transfer her to another department. Once Dr. Swim receives a letter from the provost detailing these changes, she talks to her dean, who was equally surprised by the provost's decision.

Dr. Swim, on recommendation from her dean, contacts the VP for Equity Discrimination and files a formal complaint against the provost and the senior faculty members that had accused her. The VP for Equity Discrimination contacts the legal adviser of the university to look at the allegations. The legal adviser interviewed all the faculty members in the department, and with the exception of the three senior faculty that met with the provost, none of the other members agreed that Dr. Swim had harassed them or biased them toward other faculty members.

The junior faculty also corroborated that the firing of the secretary was the right decision by Chair Swim, since she had been incompetent and had a high level of absenteeism that made her position as secretary a challenge for the faculty. The interviews went on for months, but at the end of the investigation the legal adviser supported the decisions of the provost without commenting on the senior faculty claims. Given the outcome of the university investigation, Dr. Swim decided to hire her own lawyer and sue the university and the provost.

Dr. Swim's lawyer is recognized for his reputation of working on university cases. After interviewing the faculty, the dean, and the provost, Dr. Swim's lawyer takes her case to court. At that time, the provost offers to reinstate Dr. Swim's sabbatical as well as research release time if she drops the case. Dr. Swim is most interested in having her name cleared of the harassment claims, so she decides to continue with the case.

At the writing of this case, Dr. Swim has a high probability of winning the case and the president of the university has demoted the provost.

Questions

1. Was it in the provost's purview to act without consulting the dean or actually investigating the claims?
2. What do you think of the response of the university legal adviser?
3. If you were the provost in this case, how would you have reacted to the faculty complaints?
4. Would you think that Dr. Swim has a winning case?
5. Do you think that the discrimination against Dr. Swim is in part due to the fact that she is a female?

FINAL THOUGHTS

The art of leadership is saying no, not saying yes. It is very easy to say yes.

—Tony Blair

As provost you oversee the functioning of academic affairs, but so do your deans in each college or school. So how do we interact with our deans when it comes to faculty issues? One area that always seems blurry is the support of the faculty for grants and start-ups. As provost you should recognize the achievements of faculty members and encourage faculty to excel in what they do, but remember that your dean is part of that recognition of faculty.

Another overlapping area is the provost's obligations to students, which are also the purview of faculty and deans. Maybe the best advice we can give you is that as a provost you should provide leadership rather than try to be in charge. You should be able to recognize problems and come up with creative solutions to those problems and concerns. Your job is to have a broader strategic view of things rather than being a micromanager. Effective provosts always remember that it is about others, not about them, and let deans and faculty take charge of their roles, or if the situation needs it, do the job together.

In our view, the best provosts have an open style that encourages discussion and even dissension at times, but they are also well informed on the problems of each department and their faculty. Provosts ideally work collaboratively with deans regarding well-meaning but somewhat flawed faculty initiatives to boost research productivity and classroom innovation.

Another issue that many times causes conflict between provost and deans is how to boost faculty morale. Make your faculty feel they have real power, especially when it comes to issues of budgetary cuts, but have the deans back up your initiatives. Help your faculty, along with the deans, to be creative and figuring out how to do great things with dwindling resources.

Chapter 9

The Provost's Role in Shared Governance

The provost holds the vision for the academic division, developing new programs, modeling action, communication, and good performance. Universities also see a role for faculty in decision-making on academic matters, whether through a shared governance structure or faculty union. A faculty senate/council may also inform faculty leadership about nonacademic matters that impact the academic enterprise. Issues such as space utilization, student life policies, and so on are often of major concern to faculty. We provide examples of provosts negotiating with faculty, senates, and unions for efficiency and realignment in a climate of shared governance.

WHAT IS SHARED GOVERNANCE?

We recognize that there are many different views on shared governance. Previous experiences, conversations about shared governance with colleagues, and how shared governance is handled on a provost's current campus all have an impact.

While we have a general sense of the definition of shared governance, there are many examples of misunderstanding, by both faculty and administration. Some talk about governance as the responsibility of faculty with administration being the mechanism of getting it done. Some define faculty as the "heart of the university" and believe that governance is delegated by faculty to administrators in their role as a faculty support network. Some believe that faculty and administration are inherently adversarial. In some cases, the nature of shared governance may be spelled out in the university's founding documents.

More realistically, shared governance is a balance between faculty and staff participation in planning and decision-making processes, and administrative responsibility. Historically, the system of shared governance has evolved to include more and more representation in the decision-making process. The concept appears to have come of age in the 1960s, when colleges began to liberalize many of their processes.

Shared governance is often related to a document on the subject, "Statement on Government of Colleges and Universities," which was jointly issued by the AAUP, the American Council on Education, and the Association of Governing Boards of Universities and Colleges in the mid-1960s.[1]

That statement attempted to affirm the importance of shared governance and stated some common principles. The fact that the primary organization championing faculty concerns, the body devoted to preparing future academic administrators, and the association promoting best practices in serving on governing boards together endorsed the statement illustrates that university governance is a collaborative venture.

Everyone has a role in shared governance. Various groups of people on a campus share in key decision-making processes through shared governance. Representation in these groups may be appointed or through elected representation. In some cases, certain groups are permitted to have primary responsibility for specific areas of decision-making, such as faculty for curriculum, but even there, further review is required.

Shared doesn't mean that every constituency gets to participate at every stage. Nor does it mean that any constituency exercises complete control over the process. Decision-making is not simply a function of a group vote, nor is a single person subjectively making important decisions without involving the constituents. The various stakeholders participate in well-defined parts of the process.

Faculty members traditionally exercise primary responsibility over the curriculum, because professors are the experts in their disciplines and are the best equipped to determine degree requirements and all the intricacies of a complex university curriculum. This makes sense, but even where faculty members exercise power over the curriculum, a committee vote is not the final word. At most institutions, the provost, or even the president must approve curricular changes.

As we consider these concepts, it quickly becomes apparent that shared governance is a much more difficult concept than most people anticipate. The balance between responsibility and maximum participation in decision-making is difficult to maintain. Of course, this may point to why the term

---

[1] https://www.aaup.org/report/statement-government-colleges-and-universities.

"shared governance" is frequently misused or misunderstood. Constant communication and transparency are needed to assure that all constituencies have a voice in the process, even though they don't have ultimate authority.

When the broader constituency base is invited to participate in university matters as true partners, the institution prospers. It is incumbent on a provost to be familiar with the university's shared governance processes, to be aware of the broader conversations on governance, and to seek to maintain that balance between responsibility and maximum participation in shared governance.

Scenario 1

Dr. Saiji was a provost at a private university with a strong faculty senate and a union. There were challenging times with the faculty senate, but less so with the union. Provost Saiji believed she was respectful of shared governance, so she met with the senate leadership, initially on a regular basis, and then as needed. Because the institution was in a time of growth and change, there were growing pains, and these relationships were not as "warm and fuzzy" as Provost Saiji had hoped.

Nonetheless, she believed the senate and the union were sincere contributing factors to the institution's success, even if they did not always agree about the best path forward. In her last year as provost, there was a change in the leadership of the senate. The new senate president and vice president were very much in sync with Provost Saiji and with the initiatives of academic affairs. They met every week to discuss issues at hand. The president of the senate took it upon herself to form a committee of faculty and administrators to create a "Shared Governance" document that was very successful and guides the university even today.

Scenario 2

Dr. Raham is a provost at a university that has a long and proud tradition of strong shared governance. Faculty members and faculty leaders in administrative roles are committed to ensuring that shared governance is practiced throughout academic programs, departments, schools, colleges, and the entire campus. In the university shared governance system, decisions are made through a process that rests upon collegial and collaborative consultation.

Everyone recognizes the centrality of the decision-making power of the faculty to the functioning of the university in the mission statement. For some key decisions, such as setting the unit budget or making recommendations regarding promotion or tenure, Dr. Raham as provost is required to engage in faculty consultation according to campus and university governing documents.

Furthermore, some policies dictate that particular processes be followed including faculty advice. In some cases, the input of the faculty is only advisory, and it's up to Provost Raham to be ultimately accountable for the consequences of decisions made by her unit.

In general, Dr. Raham strongly feels that the decision-making processes that include constructive, open, and honest input from all involved yield wiser decisions and, in turn, help build stronger academic units. She is also encouraged to go beyond the practices outlined in the shared governance document and to deeply integrate those principles in her dealings with her deans or the chairs of each department.

CASE 1: HOW PROVOST KRISHNA TRIED TO STRENGTHEN SHARED GOVERNANCE

Shared governance is an issue that generally attracts attention when faculties and administrations are at odds. But a sense of mutual trust and responsibility between professors and administrators can make a big difference in meeting institutional goals and carrying out campus missions. Provost Krishna's current institution had a rocky past in terms of shared governance. When she was hired as provost, her president asked her to work with the university senate and the union representatives to strengthen shared governance.

Upon meeting for more than a year on a regular basis with the faculty senate president, Provost Krishna was able to refocus the attention of the senate on actual governance, with significant results. The provost and the senate president worked collaboratively on a new GE curriculum, never an easy task. At the same time, the senate created new paths to promotion, professorial titles, and multiyear contracts for full-time faculty members off the tenure track. Colleges worked with clear guidelines for distinguishing between ranks and when promotion can occur.

Provost Krishna now has a new senate president who wants to take the senate farther, including administrators as part of the senate body, and allow the senate president to be eligible for reelection to increase stability in leadership. In her first year as provost, Dr. Krishna saw some tense moments, but she believes that the university has come a long way in strengthening shared governance. There are now excellent lines of communication, which Provost Krishna believes are key. The university has also a clear understanding of each member's role as partners and of the critical role of faculty in the oversight of academic programs.

Provost Krishna worked hard to make shared governance something that all constituencies could be proud of. She worked with the senate president to create a faculty task force to rewrite the faculty bylaws from scratch. Priorities included turning department chairs into actual department leaders with decision-making authority. Two new committees were instituted: the curriculum and assessment committee and the tenure and promotion committee.

Provost Krishna also worked with her deans in having a dean's advisory group, a five-member faculty body elected by the department chairs, to advise the dean on issues of concern. She helped to create a chairs' council that meets monthly to review policies and discuss and make recommendations on school-wide matters. In a matter of a few years, Provost Krishna created a system of shared governance that worked relatively well for the first three decades at the university.

Provost Krishna firmly believed that the process was very collegial and thorough, with town hall-style meetings to update faculty members and get their feedback. Her assessment of the success on how to achieve a successful governance reform is to do inclusively, do it very transparently, and take your time.

Questions

1. Does your institution have a good shared governance system? If not, what can you do as provost to improve it?
2. Do you agree with what Provost Krishna has done to improved shared governance at her institution?
3. Is the role of the provost to lead in shared governance?
4. What are your views on shared governance?
5. Do you have a president that is supportive of a shared governance model? What about your senate or union leaders?

Scenario 3

This scenario happened twice, at two institutions where Provost Chu worked. At his first institution, the administration and some faculty wanted to create an honors program. It was believed that an honors program would attract and retain more high-performing students. However, senior faculty tended to resist such a change as creating it would seem to reject the values for which the college stood.

Year in and year out, each time the dean and the provost would introduce the idea of initiating an honors program, the senior faculty would denounce it. Over those years, the institution was replenishing the faculty both in replacement lines and new lines. Many new faculty members were appointed. These junior faculty were of another generation, and they wanted to teach academically stronger students.

It became apparent that the more senior faculty implacably opposed an honors program and the junior faculty were all for it. Persistence paid off and an honors program was finally passed. Upon Dr. Chu's arrival as provost at his next institution, the president told him to create an honors program. The president warned Provost Chu that past efforts to start an honors program had been shot down by the faculty.

To make it happen, Provost Chu started the conversation with the junior faculty, who were invariably enthusiastic about it. By the time the senior faculty entered the conversation, the movement toward an honors program was unstoppable and it quickly passed.

CASE 2: SHARED GOVERNANCE AGONIZES OVER TECHNOLOGY FOR STUDENT SUCCESS

Provost Lubchenko is caught between various factions of shared governance. The university senate, which includes representatives from among faculty, students, and staff, has been deliberating for years on making the use of the university's Course Management System (CMS) mandatory for faculty. Staff from academic advising have been advocating for this change for years, pointing to literature that shows that when students have a uniform place in which to find all their course information, and when they can see their intermediate grades on assignments, they are more likely to take action to improve their performance.

Students have expressed anger that faculty won't use the CMS, making it more difficult for them than it was in high school, where all their course information was collected in a single spot. Yet a committee of the senate has been unable to agree on a proposal—some believe that mandating use of a CMS violates academic freedom.

Other faculty complain that the current CMS should be scrapped and a new one installed before faculty can be required to use it, and still others (particularly those who are active in the Union) are concerned that the administration will use the CMS to "spy" on faculty and retaliate against those who don't use it properly. Union leadership believes that mandatory CMS usage needs to be bargained as a condition of employment.

In conversations with faculty outside of the governance setting, Provost Lubchenko finds that many, particularly those who are newer to the university, support the "universal CMS" proposal. There appears to be a group of faculty in one college of the university who are willing to pilot the "universal CMS" proposal. The provost, jointly with representatives from the college, therefore approaches the governance committee with a plan to pilot the proposal for a full academic year, in order to collect data on how it will affect student success, how it will impact faculty work, and what technical difficulties may arise.

Since the initiative is voluntary on the part of faculty in the college, Provost Lubchenko asks the senate to suspend its deliberations on the overall proposal while the pilot runs.

The senate committee is relieved to be able to stop debating the proposal. The pilot project runs, and data on student performance suggest that the use of the CMS has had a significant impact on student retention and progression. Faculty from the pilot offer suggestions to IT on modifications to the CMS that will make it easier for them to use it. Because Provost Lubchenko has worked closely with IT, he easily gets their cooperation in implementing the modifications that are recommended, which helps increase faculty confidence in the outcome of the pilot.

By the time data on the pilot are compiled and ready to be shared with the senate, some senators on the relevant committee have stepped down and been replaced with new members. The new committee is able to review the data and make a proposal for broad implementation. The provost now sees a path to negotiate with the union, using precedents on the use of technology (such as e-mail) that have formed a basis for memoranda of understanding in past negotiations.

Questions

1. The introduction or expansion of technology often forms a nucleus for faculty resistance. What did Provost Lubchenko do to reduce such resistance? What are other strategies for easing the pain of introducing new technology into higher education?
2. What are some examples of technologies you might want to introduce at your institution?
3. Working well with IT is key to making progress in this area. How does IT interact with shared governance at your institution? To whom does IT report? Is there a faculty technology committee that is part of shared governance?

CASE 3: A PROVOST REDEFINES SHARED GOVERNANCE AFTER A MAJOR CRISIS

Provost Wilson is a very seasoned provost. Over the course of her career, she has observed two speeds of governance: foot-on-the-brake for everyday business and pedal-to-the-metal for existential decisions. She has grappled with how to honor the process of shared governance without slowing deci-sion-making to a crawl, especially in situations that require immediate action.

Many years ago, she was a member of a task force on shared governance, and she learned that the first step is to make sure that everyone understands that the sharing in "shared governance" isn't equally distributed, nor does it imply decision-making authority. That authority remains with the president and the board, who are the ones accountable for both results and shortcomings.

Provost Wilson was provost at a university that was nearly destroyed by one of the strongest hurricanes on the east coast of the United States. The university had a temporary suspension of shared governance that allowed them to recover.

Their renewal plan, which involved tremendous institutional restructuring in a short time, precluded the lengthy deliberations prescribed by normal gov-ernance procedures. But with the benefit of hindsight and another decade of experience in university leadership, Provost Wilson came to realize that what occurred after the hurricane was not the suspension of shared governance, but rather the emergence of a more effective version of shared governance.

Specifically, the Faculty Advisory Committee, a subgroup of elected rep-resentatives that assumed the university senate's powers and responsibilities, was key to what happened in the five crucial months when the university was closed after the hurricane. Schools were consolidated, several programs eliminated, and a number of staff and faculty positions terminated.

The committee members' commitment to partnering with the adminis-tration and the governing board, their constructive critiques of the propos-als, and their role as representatives of the full senate were essential to the renewal plan itself, as well as to its acceptance by the university community.

A transformation as swift and sweeping as the one Provost Wilson under-went generally seems unthinkable in higher education. What made it possible was not only a crisis that forced them to reimagine what their university could be, but also a leaner, expedited shared governance that was able to rapidly enact the decisive changes. That is, effective shared governance is not an impediment to action but a competitive advantage, one that differentiates institutions of higher education from many other organizations in both the for-profit and nonprofit sectors.

Provost Wilson's understanding of what shared governance means was honed in times of crisis. Now at her new institution, she sees the current cli-mate of uncertainty and upheaval in higher education, with public approval declining, financial stresses increasing, and social issues playing out on cam-puses, as another set of existential challenges.

She decided to send a proposal to her new president about how to reform shared governance at her new institution. She proposed what she believes is a best model, a university senate, composed of elected representatives and chaired by a president genuinely open to rational persuasion and debate that brings together diverse constituents, including faculty, staff, and students, encourages spirited dialogue, and provides a direct line to the institution's leadership, including its governing board.

Provost Wilson also recommended the creation of an executive committee of the senate, which under ordinary circumstances would periodically interact with trustees to confer on substantive issues regarding the university's future, but which would also have the authority to act quickly should the need arise.

At this point Provost Wilson is waiting for her president's decision on her two proposals on shared governance.

Questions

1. Do you think that times of crisis bring shared governance to the forefront of a university?
2. Do you agree with Provost Wilson's redefinition of shared governance after her ordeal with the hurricane?
3. Do you agree with Provost Wilson's proposal to her new president?
4. How will you propose a model of shared governance if your institution does not have one or you want to change the existing one?

CASE 4: HOW TO DEVELOP SHARED GOVERNANCE/RESPONSIBILITY

In the opinion of Provost Cuccitore, the commitment to shared governance is too often a mile wide and an inch deep. Provost Cuccitore thinks that board members, faculty leaders, and presidents praise the value of shared governance, but it frequently means something different to each of them. When that is the case, Provost Cuccitore thinks that this is the first bump in the road, because participants can become frustrated, sometimes walking away from the commitment to do the hard work of good governance. Worse yet, he thinks that when that happens, there may be mutual recriminations that can cripple an institution for years.

So, in his new job as provost, Cuccitore is proposing an effective and responsive governance, which he thinks is vitally important during times of change in higher education. In his view, shared governance in the face of sweeping and transformative change can help shift the thinking of boards, faculty, and staff from protecting yesterday's parochial interests to aligning efforts to address tomorrow's realities. When efforts are aligned, solutions are often more thoughtful and implementation time is faster.

In his proposal to the president and the BoT, Provost Cuccitore wants the creation of a Shared Governance Task Force to deliberate the following issues and came up with a strong and hopefully accepted proposal:

- Develop timely, unified, and mission-sensitive responses.
- Focus on stronger student outcomes, including better graduation rates and placement rates.
- Focus on affordability and accessibility issues requiring all members of the institution to better focus on doing their part to create the best value for an increasingly diverse set of students.

In his opening statement to the president, Provost Cuccitore proposes that to accomplish the goals of shared governance the university should move to a model of collaborative leadership, linking the president, the faculty and the BoT in a well-functioning partnership devoted to well-defined institutional vision and mission.

Provost Cuccitore thinks that when shared governance is viewed as more than a set of boundaries and rules of engagement, it can create a system where the integral leaders move beyond the fragmentation of traditional governance to shared responsibility in identifying and pursuing an aligned set of sustainable strategic directions.

Provost Cuccitore includes four practices in his proposal for the task force to consider, because he thinks that they will strengthen shared governance at his institution.

1. Actively engage board members, administrators, and faculty leaders in a serious discussion of what shared governance is and isn't.
2. Periodically assess the state of shared governance and develop an action plan to improve it.
3. Expressly support strong faculty governance of the academic program.
4. Maintain a steadfast commitment to transparency and communication.

Provost Cuccitore believes that following such practices can help his institution to build the trust and respect needed to sustain shared governance through good and bad times, since the university is moving from a traditional approach of shared governance to the more dynamic approach of shared responsibility.

After a long year and half of task force deliberations, a proposal for shared governance and shared responsibility at Provost Cuccitore's university is developed. The proposal follows most of the provost's recommendation and is strongly affirmed by the president, faculty, and BoT.

Many years later, Provost Cuccitore's university becomes a model for shared governance and shared responsibility.

Questions

1. Do you agree with the idea of shared governance/responsibility?
2. Would you follow Provost Cuccitore's advice to the task Force?
3. How would you propose a new model of shared governance/responsibility at your university?
4. What parameters would you consider?

FINAL THOUGHTS

I've learned that people will forget what you said, people will forget what you did, but people will never forget how you made them feel.

—Maya Angelou

Here are some thoughts about your role as provost on being part of shared governance:

- **Understand the role of shared governance.** Shared governance takes a village and the outcome of any project should have shared voices.
- **Bring everyone to the table.** Your team should have members with equal voices at the table, bringing them together in a cohesive forum where they feel like they have a voice to speak and a vote at the table.
- **Shared governance is about partnership, equity, accountability, and ownership among your team.** You need to have different levels of ownership and accountability on any project your team does. That partnership mindset, that idea that each one of us at the table, while not sharing the same amount of responsibility, is equally sharing the responsibility of the outcome. This allows each team member to take pride in the measures of success.
- **Track success differently for each team member, even when contributing to a single project.** Each individual that has an area of responsibility has a different measure of success and each team member has to understand what they have accountability for and what they're responsible for.

Chapter 10

Leading Change

Leading change requires having a vision for the academy. Provosts have the potential to be agents of change inside and outside of their own institutions. Provosts need to have a peer network, which can be accomplished by participating in national organizations to shape the dialogue of the future of higher education.

Being a leader is no easy task; it takes hard work, courage, and risk-taking. Being able to find solutions, solve problems, and make things better are vital components to effective leadership. Positioning yourself as a role model for people to follow means doing things that will better your students, your employees, your community, or even the world.

Scenario 1

During his tenure as provost, Dr. Stray felt that he was leading change outside his own university. He had a higher position in the boards of AAC&U, HERS, and ACAD[1]. He was able to sit at the table with leading politicians and administrators in higher education, where national policies were made.

Dr. Stray worked on the LEAP[2] program for AAC&U. He mentored many future provosts at the Harvard Institute on how to become a provost and how to implement change inside and outside their own institutions, and he also mentored many deans in how to become a provost. Dr. Stray feels that he had

---

[1] Association of American Colleges and Universities (AAC&U), Higher Education Resource Services (HERS), American Conference of Academic Deans (ACAD), respectively.
[2] Liberal Education and America's Promise (LEAP).

made multiple contributions during his career as provost, and he continued after retirement as a coach for both AAC&U and Harvard Institute.

CASE 1: TRYING TO BE AN AGENT OF CHANGE

Nearly six years ago, Dr. Abdul decided to step down as provost of his university. It was a difficult decision, but looking back at it now, he knows he made the right choice. During his tenure as provost, he led the university through difficult times, with budget cuts and political battles that had damaged the university. Provost Abdul had a new president in his last year as provost, hired specifically to move the university forward. He knew he would not be part of that next chapter.

For Dr. Abdul, it was hard to believe that it has been nearly six years since he left his administration post. He often thought that he might never return to administration. However, life as a professor was not always what he had expected at this stage of his career. As with many of his colleagues, particularly at public universities, raises were few and far between, and research funding was harder to get. Although his publications were well received, he was reaching the end of a research agenda and he wasn't sure where to turn next.

So about a year ago, Dr. Abdul made the decision to pursue an upper administration post again. He considered his options, keeping in mind that he had a wife, a teenager, and a preteen to consider as he explored possible job options. Dr. Abdul's search went back and forth across the country in his bid to find the next stop in his career. It came finally down to a couple of positions, and as fate would have it, both were in Florida, an ideal location for his wife, who as an engineer worked for NASA.

The jobs were also closer to his family. Dr. Abdul couldn't ask for a better opportunity for his family or himself. It became clear to him after interviewing which of the two jobs was a better fit for him, and although Dr. Abdul had liked being a provost, he wasn't necessarily expecting to have that opportunity again at this point in his career.

Reestablishing himself at this time and being able to lead change made him realize how lucky he was. But he also thought that it was more than just luck. He had worked very hard to get to this point in his career. Dr. Abdul is grateful to his mentors for their help, and his wife, who has been a solid supporter as they balance both family and work.

This time around, with a lot more gray hair and more savvy than in his first provost position, he was offered the position he wanted. He plans to dedicate himself to lead change at his new institution as well as within the academy as a whole. Dr. Abdul believes he has a lot to contribute, and in this time of academic turmoil, he feels it is his duty to engage with what is going on in Washington and in the direction of higher education.

Questions

1. How do you see Dr. Abdul's journey?
2. Do you think it is possible to return to the faculty after a provost position and then be viable in a provost's search? Was Dr. Abdul just lucky?
3. Had Dr. Abdul learned in his journey that he has a responsibility as an agent of change?
4. Do you think that you as a provost must be a leader in higher education? If so, how will you go about it?

CASE 2: STEPPING BACK TO THE FACULTY

Provost Starhawk had been a provost for over twelve years, after being a dean for a similar period of time. He first served at a smaller private institution, and then at a much larger and more prestigious public institution. He'd dealt multiple times with similar issues, ranging from budgets in deficit and deteriorating facilities to faculty malfeasance, student protest, legislative challenges, parental outrage, GE reform, and legislative investigations, even a major on-campus disaster.

Feeling like he'd "been there, done that," he was faced with a deep dilemma: Should he try to move up into a presidency, or was it time to go back to the faculty? Provost Starhawk's mind was deeply divided.

After months of reflection, he realized that after decades of sleepless nights, early morning emergency e-mails, heartbreaking downsizing actions, and the occasional moment of triumph, he was tired. His administrative life had coincided with many of the most difficult chapters of his personal life—a disabled child, a difficult divorce, care for his aging mother—and while he knew he had the skills to be a president, he felt less motivated to take up the 24/7 life that such a move would require.

Recently remarried to another college administrator and settled into a new home near his campus, he considered the moments of his career that had brought the most sustained satisfaction and he realized that what had motivated him from the beginning—the students themselves—was still his largest motivation. Starhawk had taught periodically during his administrative career, as a way to be sure that he was not losing touch with the very people his administration was designed to serve.

Now, when Provost Starhawk contemplated taking what he'd learned back to the classroom, he found himself getting excited. At the same time, as word that he planned to step down from his provost role spread through his campus, he was contacted by a number of newer faculty asking for mentorship and guidance. He realized that he could continue to be a leader from the "sidelines" even as he stepped back from his administrative career.

Questions

1. Many articles have been written about the dearth of qualified candidates for campus presidencies during challenging times. One of Starhawk's colleagues tells him he's "selling out" by not stepping up to a presidency. Do you think Starhawk should put aside his personal preferences to continue to serve the academy? Are there ways other than becoming a president that Starhawk can share his experience and expertise with colleagues in the academy?
2. Other options for Starhawk might have been to try his hand in the nonprofit world, where similar leadership skills are required. Have you considered administrative roles outside academia? What might be the pros and cons of such a move?
3. Starhawk taught from time to time while serving as an academic administrator. What are the advantages and disadvantages of teaching while administrating? How would you balance the need to stay in touch with students if not through teaching?
4. How do you imagine that the next provost at Starhawk's college might react to having him "leading from the sidelines" on the faculty? How might Starhawk manage the relationship with his new "boss?"

CASE 3: ASPIRING BEYOND

Provost Hanstein always aspired to be a successful, tenured professor at a teaching-centered university. Over a nearly thirty-year faculty and administrative career, she held a series of positions at two different universities, including faculty senate president, department chair, associate dean, associate provost, and provost.

In each position, Provost Hanstein discovered she enjoyed its leadership challenges, including solving difficult personnel problems, developing new policies, coping with various budget challenges, working with community stakeholders, fundraising, and collaborating with trustees. Shortly after becoming provost, she told friends and family that she could easily imagine spending the rest of her career as the chief academic officer.

In her fourth year as provost, Dr. Hanstein was taken aback when her relatively young president informed her in confidence that he would be retiring within the next two years. The president strongly suggested Dr. Hanstein should look for a presidency of her own, as Dr. Hanstein was superbly qualified for the position and clearly liked the work that makes for a successful president. The retiring president insisted that Dr. Hanstein should plan to leave her current institution, where no internal candidate had been hired as president in over fifty years and where new presidents had a history of hiring their own provosts.

Dr. Hanstein was unpleasantly surprised by this news, as she had resisted all previous pressure to consider a presidency, especially when her romantic partner currently had an excellent employment situation. Dr. Hanstein recognized, though, that her most viable choices for the next year were to seek a presidency, to find a position as provost at another university, or to return to the faculty.

She also knew that while more nontraditional candidates were becoming presidents than had once been the case, the provost's position was still the most common pathway to the presidency in American higher education. Finally, she admitted to herself that the opportunity to lead from the top appealed to her, especially given the range of skills she had developed as an administrator.

After speaking with several peers at other institutions and discussing the situation with her partner, Dr. Hanstein decided to begin applying for suitable presidencies. She found the search process rewarding at times, but she also admitted that the process was grueling, even when search consultants assured Dr. Hanstein that she was a highly competitive candidate who would eventually find the right fit. Dr. Hanstein ultimately applied for over twenty presidencies, was a semifinalist on eight occasions, and was a finalist at five different universities.

In the second year of her search, just as she began to question her decision to seek a presidency, she was offered the presidency of a regional state university in her home state. While she worried about the recent history of labor strife and racial incidents at the university, she ultimately accepted the position.

Three years later, with several important new initiatives completed or underway and a reputation established in her community for strong and principled leadership, President Hanstein was sure she had made the right decision. While rewarding in its own way, the provost's position also had given her the depth of executive knowledge and experience that allowed her to succeed in her new role. She also was careful to give the provost at her new institution the authority and support the provost needed in order to lead effectively.

Questions

1. Do you think Dr. Hanstein made the right decision becoming a president? Is a presidency the best way to share a provost's experience and expertise?
2. Did the fact that Dr. Hanstein had a supportive partner make her decision easier? Should her partner have opposed the move, what other options might Dr. Hanstein have had?
3. Do you support Dr. Hanstein's decision to provide leadership roles for her new provost? Would you do the same?
4. If you feel a presidency is in your future, what experience do you feel you need to be a successful candidate?

FINAL THOUGHTS

I start with the premise that the function of leadership is to produce more leaders, not more followers.

—Ralph Nader

Leadership plays a key role in successful change efforts. Change requires skill and will. Useful change is never employed effectively unless it is driven by high-quality leadership, not just excellent management. Strong leadership can motivate the actions needed to alter behavior in any significant way. Strong leadership can get change to stick by anchoring it in the very culture of an organization.

Leadership is the engine that drives change. Successful transformations do not happen on their own; they must be led. For change efforts to be successful, behaviors must be altered. If behavior isn't altered, we're doomed to repeat past mistakes. Everyone has a stake in orchestrating change in their organization. Real transformations take time. Change sticks when it becomes *"the way we do things around here."*

Transformation requires sacrifice, dedication, and creativity. Change is not easy; don't underestimate how hard it is to drive people out of their comfort zones. People will not make sacrifices, even if they are unhappy with the status quo, unless they think the potential benefits of change are attractive and unless they really believe that a transformation is possible. Leading successful change is probably one of the most important responsibilities of your leadership role.

References and Further Reading

American Association of State Colleges and Universities. n.d. "Becoming a Provost Academy." Accessed December 1, 2019. https://aascu.org/LD/BAPA/.

American Association of University Professors. n.d. "Statement on Government of Colleges and Universities." Accessed July 10, 2019. https://www.aaup.org/report/statement-government-colleges-and-universities.

American Council on Education. 2014. *2013–14 CAO Census Survey.* Accessed November 30, 2019. https://www.acenet.edu/Documents/Chief-Academic-Officer-Survey-CAO-Professional-Pathways.pdf.

Borwick, John. March 11, 2013. "What is a Provost? An Introduction to Administrative and Academic Ranks." *Higher Education IT Management.* http://www.heitmanagement.com/blog/2013/03/what-is-a-provost-an-introduction-to-administrative-and-academic-ranks/.

Boulgarides, James and William Cohen. 2001. "Leadership style vs. leadership tactics." *Journal of Applied Management and Entrepreneurship*, 6(1): 59–73.

Bugeja, Michael. February 14, 2018. "What do Provosts and Deans Actually do?" *Inside Higher Ed.* https://www.insidehighered.com/views/2018/02/14/poorly-defined-roles-provosts-and-deans-can-lead-problems-major-universities.

Buller, Jeffrey L. 2013. *Essential Academic Leadership: How to Stop Putting Out Fires and Start Making a Difference.* San Francisco: Jossey-Bass.

Buller, Jeffrey L. 2015. *The Essential Academic Dean or Provost: A Comprehensive Desk Reference.* 2nd ed. San Francisco: Jossey-Bass.

Carlson, Scott. 2019. "Why Being a Provost is one of the Toughest Jobs at Vulnerable Colleges." *Chronicle of Higher Education.* November 8, 2019.

Clayton, Victoria. 2019. "Provost: help wanted." *University Business*, 22(5): 17–21.

Clayton, Victoria. June 18, 2019. "Expanding the Role of the Chief Academic Officer." *University Business.* https://universitybusiness.com/7-ways-the-provosts-job-is-bigger-and-broader-than-ever-before/.

Cohen, William. 2000. *The New Art of the Leader: Leading with Integrity and Honor.* Paramus, New Jersey: Prentice Hall Press, 2000.

Ehrenberg, Ronald G., George H. Jakubson, Mirinda L. Martin, Joyce B. Main, and Thomas Eisenberg. "Diversifying the faculty across gender lines: Do trustees and administrators matter?" *Economics of Education Review*, 31(1): 9–18.

Gardner, Lee. 2015. "The path to change runs through the provost's office." *Chronicle of Higher Education*, 62(2): 16.

Inside Higher Ed. 2020. "The 2020 Survey of College and University Chief Academic Officers." https://www.insidehighered.com/booklet/2020-survey-college-and-un iversity-chief-academic-officers.

Julius, Daniel. December 2, 2016. "On Being a Provost: Four Simple Truths about a Complex Role." The Evolllution. https://evolllution.com/managing-institution/ operations_efficiency/on-being-a-provost-four-simple-truths-about-a-complex -role/.

Keller, Morton and Keller, Phyllis. 2001. *Making Harvard Modern: The Rise of America's University*. New York: Oxford University Press.

Kouzes, James and Barry Posner. 2010. *The Leadership Challenge*. New York: Jossey-Bass, A Wiley Company.

Lencioni, Patrick. 2004. *Death by Meeting: A Leadership Fable*. New York: Jossey-Bass, A Wiley Company.

Maghroori, Ray and Charles Powers. August 2, 2007. "Vice President vs. Provost." *Chronicle of Higher Education*. https://www.chronicle.com/article/Vice-Presid ent-vs-Provost/46483.

Martin James, James E. Samuels, and Associates, eds. 2015. *The Provost's Handbook: The Role of the Chief Academic Officer*. Baltimore: Johns Hopkins University Press.

Mitchell, Brian C. and W. Joseph King. 2018. *How to Run a College: A Practical Guide for Trustees, Faculty, Administrators, and Policymakers*. Baltimore: Johns Hopkins University Press.

Murrell, Lisa E. and Aaron W. Hughey. 2003. "The Effects of job attributes, institutional mission emphasis, and institution type on perceptions of the provost position." *Educational Administration Quarterly*, 39(4): 533–565.

Nielson, Larry A. 2019. *Provost: Experiences, Reflections and Advice from a Former "Number Two" on Campus*. Sterling, VA: Stylus Publishing.

Raelin, Joseph. 2003. *Creating Leaderful Organizations: How to Bring out Leadership in Everyone*. San Francisco: Berrett-Koehler Publishers.

Rothwell, William and Peter Chee. 2013. *Becoming an Effective Mentoring Leader*. New York: McGraw Hill Publishers.

Stevenson, Joseph. 2000. "The modern university provost". *Education*, 121(2): 347–350.

Stewart, M. Concetta. January 28, 2019. "The Elusive (and Expanding) Role of the Provost." *Higher Ed Jobs*. https://www.higheredjobs.com/articles/articleDisplay.cf m?ID=1815.

Swindall, Clint. 2011. *Engaged Leadership: Building a Culture to Overcome*. New Jersey: John Wiley and Son Publishers.

About the Authors

Dr. Patricia Mosto has a PhD in environmental sciences. She studied at Drexel University, the University of Texas at Austin, and the University of Buenos Aires, Argentina. She has been actively involved with projects related to water quality and water pollution issues for the last fifty years. Dr. Mosto joined the Department of Biological Sciences at Rowan University in 1993. In her academic career, she was the chair of the Biological Sciences Department, the Interim Associate Provost for Academic Affairs, and the associate dean for the College of Liberal Arts and Sciences. She joined Rider University as the dean of the College of Liberal Arts, Education, and Sciences in 2009 and retired in 2016. She has published four books and chapters in another five books, over fifty articles in peer-reviewed journals, and over fifty peer-reviewed technical reports. She has presented her research at local, national, and international conferences. She currently teaches at Northern Virginia Community College.

Dr. Gail M. Simmons holds a BS in Biological Sciences from the University of Pittsburgh and a PhD in Genetics from the University of California at Davis. She spent four years as a Staff Fellow at the National Institution of Environmental Health Sciences in North Carolina before joining the faculty of the Department of Biology of the City College of the City University of New York (CUNY) in 1989. Her research on the molecular evolution of transposable genetic elements in Drosophila has been published in major journals and she has served as associate editor of the *Journal of Molecular Evolution*. While at City College she was active in promoting research opportunities for underserved students and in developing interdisciplinary approaches to science education. This work led to her first administrative position, as associate dean of the Division of Science at City College. Dr. Simmons served as dean of Science at the College of New Jersey, and then as dean of Science and Technology at the College of Staten Island of CUNY. She went on to serve as provost at two New York institutions—Manhattanville College and Hofstra University. During her nearly ten years as a provost, she also presented at national conferences and consulted on accreditation, personnel issues, and curriculum issues. She has returned to her first love, teaching science to non-science majors, in the Biology department at Hofstra University.

Dr. Brian McGee has a PhD in communication. He studied at Southern Illinois University-Carbondale and Ohio State University. His research interests have included argumentation, political communication, and rhetoric and racism. Dr. McGee's earliest faculty appointments were at Northeast Louisiana University and Texas Tech University. He later served as the chair of the School of Communication at Spalding University and the chair of the Department of Communication at the College of Charleston. At the College of Charleston, Dr. McGee went on to hold appointments as chief of staff and senior vice president for Executive Administration and as provost and executive vice president of Academic Affairs. He has published over twenty-five book chapters and peer-reviewed articles and presented his research at numerous regional, national, and international conferences, in addition to his service as editor of Contemporary Argumentation and Debate. Dr. McGee currently serves as president of Quincy University.

Dr. Dianne Dorland has a PhD in chemical engineering. She received her BS and MS from South Dakota School of Mines and Technology and began her career with Union Carbide Corporation and then Dupont as a process engineer. Returning to academia, she holds a PhD in chemical engineering from West Virginia University in mid-career. Dr. Dorland was one of the initial faculty appointed at the University of Minnesota Duluth to start a chemical engineering department. She served for fourteen years, ten of which as department head before being recruited to serve as dean of Engineering at Rowan University. During her twelve years at Rowan, Dr. Dorland served on the Board of Directors for the American Institute of Chemical Engineers (AIChE) and was elected president of the 40,000 member professional society. She has served on numerous boards bringing business applications to engineering. Dr. Dorland has retired and transitioned to public education as a certified University of Minnesota Extension Master Gardener with a focus on safe pesticide use.